The Complete Guide to Google AdWords

Secrets, Techniques, and Strategies You Can Learn to Make Millions

By Larisa Lambert

THE COMPLETE GUIDE TO GOOGLE ADWORDS: SECRETS, TECHNIQUES, AND STRATEGIES YOU CAN LEARN TO MAKE MILLIONS

Copyright © 2011 Atlantic Publishing Group, Inc.
1405 SW 6th Avenue • Ocala, Florida 34471 • Phone 800-814-1132 • Fax 352-622-1875
Web site: www.atlantic-pub.com • E-mail: sales@atlantic-pub.com
SAN Number: 268-1250

Library of Congress Cataloging-in-Publication Data

Lovelady, Larisa, 1968-
  The complete guide to Google AdWords : secrets, techniques, and strategies you can learn to make millions / Larisa Lovelady.
     p. cm.
  Includes bibliographical references and index.
  ISBN 978-1-60138-318-1 (alk. paper)
  1. Google AdWords. 2. Internet marketing. I. Title.
  HF5415.1265.L68 2010
  659.14'4--dc22
                         2010033250

PROJECT MANAGER: Nicole Orr • EDITOR: Brad Goldbach
FRONT COVER DESIGN: Meg Buchner • megadesn@mchsi.com
BACK COVER: Jacqueline Miller • millerjackiej@gmail.com

Printed in the United States

Printed on Recycled Paper

We recently lost our beloved pet "Bear," who was not only our best and dearest friend but also the "Vice President of Sunshine" here at Atlantic Publishing. He did not receive a salary but worked tirelessly 24 hours a day to please his parents. Bear was a rescue dog that turned around and showered myself, my wife, Sherri, his grandparents Jean, Bob, and Nancy, and every person and animal he met (maybe not rabbits) with friendship and love. He made a lot of people smile every day.

We wanted you to know that a portion of the profits of this book will be donated to The Humane Society of the United States. —*Douglas & Sherri Brown*

The human-animal bond is as old as human history. We cherish our animal companions for their unconditional affection and acceptance. We feel a thrill when we glimpse wild creatures in their natural habitat or in our own backyard.

Unfortunately, the human-animal bond has at times been weakened. Humans have exploited some animal species to the point of extinction.

The Humane Society of the United States makes a difference in the lives of animals here at home and worldwide. The HSUS is dedicated to creating a world where our relationship with animals is guided by compassion. We seek a truly humane society in which animals are respected for their intrinsic value, and where the human-animal bond is strong.

Want to help animals? We have plenty of suggestions. Adopt a pet from a local shelter, join The Humane Society and be a part of our work to help companion animals and wildlife. You will be funding our educational, legislative, investigative and outreach projects in the U.S. and across the globe.

Or perhaps you would like to make a memorial donation in honor of a pet, friend or relative? You can through our Kindred Spirits program. And if you would like to contribute in a more structured way, our Planned Giving Office has suggestions about estate planning, annuities, and even gifts of stock that avoid capital gains taxes.

Maybe you have land that you would like to preserve as a lasting habitat for wildlife. Our Wildlife Land Trust can help you. Perhaps the land you want to share is a backyard — that's enough. Our Urban Wildlife Sanctuary Program will show you how to create a habitat for your wild neighbors.

So you see, it is easy to help animals. And The HSUS is here to help.

2100 L Street NW • Washington, DC 20037 • 202-452-1100
www.hsus.org

Dedication & Acknowledgements

This book is dedicated to my parents, Joe and Jo Ann Lambert. Thank you.

Acknowledgements

Much thanks, love, and appreciation go to my family and friends for your support, encouragement, and prayers in helping me complete this book. My husband, Scott, deserves much credit for his support, help in the kitchen, Red Bull deliveries, emergency neck rubs, and everything else that he did to help me have some uninterrupted time in a household full of three active boys. To my sons, Vann, Joseph, and Jack, I could not have continued to research and type many times without your hugs, grins, and your belief that I am capable of so much. Thankfully, I have too many friends to mention here individually who lent their support to me in so many ways for this, my first book of many.

Thank you specifically to Tom Prewett for your insight, feedback, and constructive criticism to help make this book better for its target audience.

A special thank you goes to Dr. John Wittig of the Department of Communication Studies at University of Alabama at Birmingham for allowing me to teach the basics of Google™ AdWords to one of his classes. The feedback was invaluable.

For those that helped me make this happen at Atlantic Publishing Group, especially Nicole Orr for her positive and constructive editorial prowess, I pass along my gratitude.

To Tim Kassouf, thanks so much for lending your professionalism and your AdWords experience and expertise to help make this guide to Google AdWords complete.

Above all, thanks to the One who is my Author and Finisher, and the Giver of All Good Things.

Table of Contents

Chapter 3: What Do I Need to Know About My Business to Get Started?   61

Chapter 4: Branding Your Organization for More Effective AdWords Results   95

Chapter 7: What Do I Do to Get Started? 169

Chapter 12: How do I Make the System Work Better? 261

Conclusion 275

Appendix: Web site Resources 279

Bibliography 281

Author Biography 283

Index 285

Introduction

"Do you use Google AdWords to promote your business?"

"Um, well, I use Google to find information to help my business, but what is AdWords?"

This is the typical response I have received in conversations about this book — conversations I have had with business owners, managers, non-profit employees; and marketing, advertising, and public relations professionals. These are people who work hard to promote their businesses, yet are unfamiliar with Google's marketing-made-easy approach, something that can save a remarkable amount of time and money.

Most people I have spoken with use Google to search the Internet and are aware of the ads that run along the side of their search queries, but have no idea how they are placed, how much they cost, or how to go about getting an ad for their business. Assumptions include the notions that:

- whoever pays the most gets the top ad spot
- advertising on Google would cost too much
- only advertisers trying to advertise worldwide should buy these ads.

All of these assumptions are incorrect. You can spend as much or as little on a Google advertising campaign as your budget allows, and you can customize your campaign in a variety of ways, including limiting where it appears. Did you notice I said Google "campaign," not just Google "ad?" That is right. With Google advertising, you can run multiple campaigns that include lots of ads, and it is not that difficult or that expensive. AdWords is the fastest growing advertising program on the market. It would not continue to grow if it did not work. Teaching you how to make it work for your business or organization is my goal for this book.

I have owned a small business since 1997 and, simultaneously, have worked full-time, promoting everything from restaurants to nonprofits to cable TV to orthodontic services. I have been fortunate to work with business owners, managers, technicians, customer service personnel, accountants, volunteers, and lots and lots of customers. From all of these people, I have learned that most people want to succeed. Although their definitions of success have a broad range, most people want to make their lives better. Many entrepreneurs and founders of nonprofits, or service organizations, launch into the public world to offer something they do well or that they believe is worthy. Few of them envision mediocrity, or even failure. Being able to promote a business successfully causes a ripple effect that improves the lives of owners, managers, employees, and customers.

The goal of this book is to further your success. By understanding and thoughtfully using marketing tools and opportunities, your business or organization can move forward to the excellence you envision.

The most gifted, trustworthy provider of a seldom-used service is not effective as a service provider because the service is not used. Your organization may offer solutions that meet the needs of millions, but if you are unable to attract volunteers, or those who desperately need these solutions, your solutions are not valued. The availability of your revolutionary product could provide income for you, your family, and the employees you will hire. If no one knows they can purchase this amazing product, it will not contribute to your income — or anyone else's.

The entire free market economy is based on getting the word out and making an exchange. If you do not get the word out, the exchange will not be made. Millions of dollars are spent on getting the word out. Millions of dollars are made because the word is presented to the people willing to make an exchange. Never before has getting the word out to the right people been so simple and affordable. Effective advertising can be costly. Often, the more effective the advertising opportunity, the more costly it is. Advertising on network television can cost tens of thousands of dollars. It works because a lot of people see the message. But, if you do not have that kind of money to promote your business, it does not work for you. The advent of the Internet, and, specifically, the Google AdWords program, presents advertising opportunities that can easily become a part of your advertising strategy, or that can become the entire focus of your marketing budget and efforts.

Learning the specific components of Google AdWords, its related services, and how all of the components work together to create a user-friendly revenue opportunity, will help you use AdWords for optimal performance for your business or organization. AdWords contains an amazing number of options. I will outline these options in this book so you can make fully informed decisions about how each may affect your ad or campaign; therefore, your business' bottom line. AdWords allows you to create an ad, determine where it is displayed on the Google network, and then bring Google users to your site, where you can convert these users to customers. Once they arrive at your site, you can also collect valuable information you can use to find new customers and keep current customers coming back for more.

AdWords also provides a number of analytical tools to help you maximize the effectiveness of your advertising. You can easily make changes based on the information they provide, and you will learn how to use these tools to increase your revenue.

You do not have to be an advertising, marketing, or public relations professional to understand how to produce campaigns and analyze the results. This book will walk beginners through the step-by-step process of analyzing your business or organization, determining what advertising methods will benefit you the most, implementing a realistic strategy, and analyzing the success of your efforts.

AdWords uses the same fundamental principles as successful, traditional, offline marketing. Concise, targeted messages are used to grab attention and move Google users to your website. AdWords then calculates how many times your ad is shown, and how many times users click on your ad, going a step beyond offline advertising.

For those already schooled in promoting goods and services, this back-to-basics approach will serve as a reminder of how things ought to be, as well as a source of fresh ideas about effectively using Google AdWords to cross-promote campaigns and conduct inexpensive market tests. Use this book as a training tool for other departments in your company that need to understand why you do what you do, or why you ask so many questions. Use it to help keep your brilliant creative strategies grounded, and to help you stay focused on what is most important — getting the right message to the right people at the right time, thus affecting their tendency to favor your product over that of your competitor.

The book is divided into three sections so you can find information based on where you are in the process of using AdWords. *The first section, Before You Begin, helps you understand the basics of the AdWords program and takes an in-depth look at your business to determine how AdWords can work best to increase your revenue.* The concepts in this section are fundamental to the growth and profitability of any business and will serve as a base for everything you do in AdWords. You will learn how to set measurable goals and objectives and why they are important. You will learn how to look at your business as a business — not as a hobby, and not as an obligation. These principles will empower you to operate your business, nonprofit, department, or individual job from a measurable, productive point of view. This will also include budgeting for all of your company's resources and the process of comprehensively branding your organization, and how AdWords can help you accomplish this important perception-based factor that can help your business succeed.

Like many systems, processes, ideas, and organizations, online advertising has its own vocabulary. You will learn the basic terms for the AdWords language and be able to understand them within the context of your ads, campaigns, and their results. Knowing the terms and being able to apply them can be quite different. We will also look at the components of the AdWords system and show you how the whole thing works together so that you understand the context, the reasons, and the possibilities for decisions you make regarding your ads and campaigns. After reading this section, you should fully understand how the AdWords system can work for your unique situation. You will know which components you want to implement immediately, and those you may want to file for future reference.

To help make these terms, and the rest of this book's information, as relevant as possible, we are going to use a hypothetical example of a company working hard to sell its product. This company's goal is for its products to "sell like hotcakes." To keep these examples light, and just a little corny, our imaginary company is going to actually sell hotcakes online. That is right, we are going to sell hotcakes like, well, hotcakes — through a Google AdWords campaign. As you move through the steps of understanding, developing, implementing, and maintaining your own AdWords campaigns, the little hotcakes company will be moving through the process right along with you and will help you view options and make decisions based on information that all real-life organizations need.

In the second section, Getting Set Up, you will learn how to establish your AdWords account successfully from the beginning, using the concepts, ideas, and understanding you have gained from the rest of the book to do this efficiently. You will learn how to research, choose, and bid on words and phrases that correspond to your product and services, called keywords, that will be used to trigger your ad's appearance on Google. You will learn how to write an effective ad and create a page on the Web where customers will go to give you more information or to buy your product. You will also learn about Google's tools to help you do this. You will learn what they are and how and when to use them most effectively.

Section three, Your Ads Appear, teaches you to understand how your ads are performing and how to increase their performance. It also focuses on optimizing your online presence through Google and all of its business solutions, and how they can work together to affect your bottom line. This section also looks at other Internet advertising options, as well as traditional offline options, so that you can make informed decisions on whether to broaden your scope of marketing through other sources.

The case studies, examples, worksheets, and quizzes included throughout this book will give you real-life examples of others use Google AdWords and will ease your entry into the AdWords arena. These informational, reusable, and customizable tools alone are worth the cost of this book. Of course, I encourage you to read every word, but I understand that my editor and my mom may be my only two shots at that. That is fine with me, as long as the information that you do get is practical and easy to implement within your unique situation.

In short, we will look at where you are, where you want to be, and the best ways to get there. No matter where you are in the business cycle — from pre-launch to established — the information in this book will give you the tools to determine if there is truly a market for your new product, to help you gain more customers, or to help you keep the customers that you have.

SECTION 1

Before You Begin

Many businesses fail because of undercapitalization, which means they do not have the startup money to allow themselves time to grow until they are profitable. Many businesses fail because the owner is really great at something and passionate about offering this to customers and doing this for a living. This does not sound like a bad thing, and it is not, but running a successful business requires knowledge about running a business. In order to succeed, the talented, passionate business owner must understand how to offer goods or services in the context of the business world. That is what this section is all about. Running a successful AdWords campaign can be an important component in growing and operating a healthy business. This section will help you understand more about what successful businesses do to stay successful.

How to Use This Information

As a business owner and long-time marketing professional, I have marketed a diverse range of businesses and organizations and share with you many fundamental and advanced techniques for getting the word out about your product, your service, or your organization. Every campaign I have worked on has been executed perfectly with astounding results. Well, not exactly, but that was a fun little fantasy. Professionals in every field make mistakes in judgment and execution, and I am certainly no exception to that rule.

The wonderful thing about trying to sell a product, a service, or an idea, is that ads or campaigns considered to be a flop often reveal information about your customers that you really need to know in order to provide them with what they need, and more important, what they are willing to act on. With Google AdWords, the turnaround time for transforming the concept for an ad or a campaign into a results-driven component of your business is greatly reduced. You can have an idea for an ad, write it, post it in minutes, and analyze its effectiveness within hours.

Saving time saves resources, which saves money. As part of the marketing team for a large telecommunications company, one of my responsibilities was to set the parameters for information that would be captured for each sale generated by our marketing and advertising efforts. When I first started doing this, it would require at least two meetings with members of our information technology (IT) department, and the language barrier between marketing and the billing system that generated the information was highly frustrating for all of us. My learning curve was painful because I knew what I wanted was possible; I just did not know how to make it happen. After much patience (and quite a bit of sighing) in response to my questions, we worked together to understand the needs of each department. The cost for the time it took us to reach the point of understanding and work together to meet the needs of our marketing efforts was an important investment, but it was expensive. That cost was very real, considering the time we took for meetings and planning, not to mention the cost of our unsuccessful efforts to obtain the data we needed. If you added up our hourly wages and multiplied that by the amount of time we spent on meetings, then added the cost of printing and postage for mail pieces that went to the wrong house, plus the money lost on not gaining the customers we needed for each campaign, the bill for this learning curve in blending marketing and analytics would be substantial. But with Google AdWords, a balanced blend of marketing and analytics is available, and it does not require a degree or prior experience to be used effectively.

Aside from helping to keep your time investment relatively low, the financial investment in your campaign can also be closely controlled and, therefore, kept relatively low when compared with other long-established advertising outlets. With AdWords, budgeting is up to you. If you have $100 to spend or $100 million, you can develop your own campaign to fit your budget. Many other advertising media require a deposit, and have minimum cost requirements that you may not be able to meet. AdWords is able to keep costs low because the Internet is fueled by content from millions of sources. Google does not have the same overhead costs associated with most offline advertising media, such as the cost of paper for printing direct mail, magazines, or newspapers. Google also is not required to pay rent for using infrastructure as cable companies are required to do in order to attach the cable lines to poles owned by power companies. Google certainly has costs that go with any business, but its situation is unique. It has maintained consistency in passing along costs only as its advertisers incur them.

If you do not have a marketing plan, use this book to guide you in developing a plan that includes the easy-to-use, online technology of AdWords. Marketing, sales, or public relations goals can make an enormous difference in results. Rather than saying yes to an advertiser who calls you persistently just because you know you need to somehow get the word out about your product or service, you can verify an advertiser's effectiveness as it relates to your plan. You will be armed with the knowledge of what advertising should accomplish for your business and be prepared to negotiate pricing and timing to get the maximum return on your advertising dollar investment. Getting comfortable with AdWords will take some thought, and some time. The time spent to research and prepare your ads and campaigns before you post your first ad is a worthy investment in fully understanding what your audience is looking for, and how to present yourself to that audience.

It is also exciting to think that you can use the information here to immediately jump into a Google AdWords campaign and test it while you discover other ways to improve your campaign and, consequently, make your business better. You can easily use the information in this book to start an AdWords campaign right now. Within all of Google's Business Solutions, including AdWords, you will find a variety of helpful resources, including user discussions, blogs, helpful articles, and information on seminars. Google is responsive to feedback and analysis from its users and is continually enlarging the online resources found within the AdWords program. You can use this book as a reference for AdWords tat any phase of your AdWords experience. Read it first to understand what you are doing in AdWords, and why each step is important to a successful ad campaign. Or, read it as you go through each step of the AdWords process. If you are already an AdWords user, read it to make the most of the AdWords revenue opportunity and to expand your business in the direction you have determined it needs to go.

The help section for Google AdWords is extensive, but finding some of the information is difficult. If you do not know the information is there, you do not know to look for it. Google's help section is continuously changing. It contains videos, definitions, articles, a help forum, access to free AdWords Webinars, a blog, information on technical issues, troubleshooting tips, a Beginner's Guide, and a Learning Center, which contains information in both interactive and text formats. All of the information you need to operate a successful Google AdWords campaign is available there, if you can find it. This book is an easy-to-navigate companion "guide to the guide" for contextual information and examples of how to best utilize this powerful advertising tool.

Feel free to jump around through this book. Just as your ads and campaigns should be customized to your target audience, this book can easily be customized to you; it was written with your needs in mind. And, as the needs of each of your customers are slightly different, I understand that each of my readers needs information in different formats, presented in different ways to use for different goals, so I will repeat information to make sure you absorb the most important points, and I will use lots of screen shots, bullet points, and boxes to highlight information in an easy-to-find and remember format.

Please note that AdWords is continually evolving and, as of this writing, these terms and their definitions are up-to-date.

Chapter One

What is a Google AdWord and How Does it Apply to Me?

AdWords is Google's advertising system that may be used to create an ad that appears within the Google business solutions system, determine how often and where it will appear, and measure the results of the ad. Multiple ads may be managed within campaigns, and multiple campaigns may be managed within AdWords. AdWords is designed to be user-friendly and simple. You pay for ads on AdWords only if they are clicked, or selected, by a user on the Google network of sites. Or, you may pay for every time an ad appears within Google's myriad advertising options. Because Google wants your advertising to be successful so you continue to use the AdWords program, AdWords offers a variety of tools and solutions to optimize the attraction and effectiveness of your ads.

The basics of how a potential customer, referred to here as a "clicker," accesses your ad through the AdWords system is shown in the diagram on the next page:

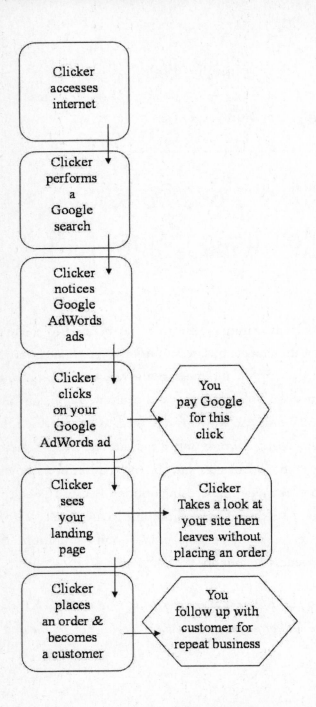

Brief History of Google AdWords

Google, Inc., the online search engine company created by Stanford University students Sergey Brin and Larry Page, experienced explosive growth after its founding in 1998. In June 2000, Google became the world's largest search engine when its search index reached 1 billion URLs. Just four months later, Google launched Google AdWords. At the time of the launch, Google, Inc., reported "widespread adoption" of the AdWords program during its worldwide beta test, during which the company allowed a small group of 350 advertising agencies and businesses to use the product before it was released for public distribution.

At the time of the launch, AdWords was touted as a self-service advertising system simple to use for every business. Its simplicity came from making an advertising solution available to anyone with a computer and Internet access. The system continues to be simple to use. However, its simplicity for the user comes from honing complex systems and statistics into easily understandable language and an easily adjustable format. Google AdWords has succeeded in making the complex simple. By going to one Web site, you can customize ads, campaigns, schedule, pause, place, and get results that might otherwise require numerous phone calls, spreadsheets, and production schedules.

Google AdWords has done for advertising analysis what modern ovens have done for a bread baker. Same result: smells good, tastes good, and gives you energy, but without chopping or gathering firewood yourself — you just turn it on to pre-heat, then bake. The AdWords analytical tools use the same ingredients for its analysis: time consuming research and traditional analysis benchmarks, such as return on investment, cost per sale, and results percentages. Once the ingredients — your keywords, ads, placement, and budget — are mixed together, just click your AdWords account summary to determine the effectiveness of your campaign.

AdWords was started based on Google's foundation of excellence in the Internet search arena. Google's primary mission is to be a search engine that organizes the world's information in an accessible, user-friendly manner. The relevance it places in its formula for ranking ads, placing ads, and helping you find appropriate keywords is an integral part of its success.

During a recent Internet search, I did a search using a competitor of Google. After I found the information I needed on the cooking site, I glanced at the ads displayed on the page. They were all related to auto repair. A cooking site with auto repair ads is an interesting combination. The auto repair advertisers had a 0 percent chance that I would click on their ad for more information because I was searching for cooking information, not auto repair information. The auto repair information was irrelevant. Relevance matters, and it is the foundation of the AdWords program.

AdWords for you today

Fox News reported Google as the number one search engine in the world in November 2009. The company earned more than 22 billion dollars in advertising revenue, or more than two-thirds of all U.S. newspaper ad revenue.

Unlike many advertising mediums, AdWords does not require you to sign a contract and is customizable. This allows you to freely drop, change, and add to campaigns or individual ads in a specific time frame, and with a budget that best meets your business' needs. With AdWords, there is no free trial period — just monthly charges. You pay a $5 account activation fee, and then pay for the responses to your ad, which are measured by how many users see them or click on them.

As part of the marketing department for a large company, I poured hours into researching and developing a campaign, thinking, "This is my chance to really impress the boss and get more customers." The campaign was scheduled to launch on broadcast television on Sept. 12, 2001. In the aftermath of the September 11 terrorist attacks, every channel covered the breaking news, and, rightfully so, no one cared about my broadcast campaign. The ads did not run, but we had to pay for their production. I lost all the investment of time and energy that went into the campaign. I was unable to react instantly to changes in the marketplace that made my entire campaign completely irrelevant. Because the campaign was time sensitive in promoting a specific product, I could not re-purpose it for later use. Besides the frustration this caused me, it cost the company thousands of dollars. Unlike many other advertising venues, Google AdWords makes it quick and easy to react to these types of changes in the marketplace.

With AdWords, you can create an ad within minutes to respond to a competitor's price shift, or to a newsworthy event. If a particular product you sell is put on back order from your supplier, put its ad on hold. If you realize that you have surplus inventory of a particular product, adjust your campaign to offer new customers a deeper discount that keeps them coming back for more. If news headlines address a service you offer, change your keywords and Content Network options to associate with the news stories (or move yourself out of the radar of negative press). With Google AdWords, you have flexibility and options to adjust your ads and campaigns quickly to react offensively or defensively to the marketplace.

In the summer of 2009, Google introduced a new AdWords interface, appropriately named the 2009 Interface. If you are new to AdWords, what changed really does not matter as much as how the results of the changes affect your new AdWords account. Before the 2009 Interface was implemented, AdWords users were able to select from either a Starter Edition account or a Standard Edition account. With the new interface, everyone will use the same edition. The blend of the two editions makes it easier to use AdWords. When you are first starting out with the program, keep your ad and campaign options simple. Then, you decide when you are ready to access more advanced features. There is now no need to graduate to a more advanced edition because the only edition available allows you to use both simple and advanced options. If you hear or see references to the Starter or Standard Edition of AdWords online or in AdWords help, understand that the two have blended.

The ability to change an entire advertising campaign in just a few minutes is astounding compared to the lead times necessary for many other types of advertising, such as special events, print, and broadcast media. AdWords is also multidimensional, flexible, and easily scaled, so that businesses and organizations of any type and size can use it effectively.

AdWords, and its continual developments, makes it easy for you, the non-profit volunteer, the small business owner, or the marketing professional, to fully execute a single ad or an entire advertising campaign all by yourself. With AdWords, it is also possible for you to easily become the customer. It is common with direct mail and telemarketing campaigns to include an employee's contact information as a "plant" or "test" address or phone number to verify that the mailer was received in homes on the target date. To do this, you would include, or "plant," your mailing address or phone number in the list of those receiving the mailer or the phone calls. It is also fun to catch a broadcast or cable ad that you created as it shows on a top-rated television show, or to hear a radio spot that you wrote and scheduled during your own morning drive time. However, in many of those cases, you are not the target audience and would not receive the advertising message if you did not already know when it was scheduled. With AdWords, you can do a search for your keywords and look at the results yourself. Of course, your AdWords account gives you the information on your ad's impressions, or how often it shows up when someone searches Google for one of your keywords. It also gives information on Web pages that may include your ad. It is easy to schedule your own test. Just do a search the way your potential customer would do a search. Go to **www.google.com**, type one of your keywords into the search window, and check out the ads that appear along with the results of the search. This is also a great way to check out your competition's ads. You can easily view the context of your ads on specific sites, news pages, blogs, or online communities.

Some of the specific things you can do by using AdWords as an integral part of your advertising strategy include:

- Create an ad that will appear on the Web.
- Select where that ad will be shown.
- Research keywords to reach your target market.
- Set up target markets based on location and a variety of other options.
- Use different types of ads including text ads, image ads, video ads, and more.
- Set your own AdWords budget.
- Bid on keywords that may increase interest in your ad.
- Select payment options.
- Set up campaigns to manage multiple ads.
- Analyze how individual ads and campaigns are performing.
- Quickly and easily change ads and campaigns.

Some of the possible effects of AdWords on your business include:

- increased profitability

- the ability to explore new products and services inexpensively

AdWords as Part of Your Advertising Efforts

With Google, you can use multiple advertising and promotion opportunities. *For more information about other Google opportunities, see Chapter 5.*

- AdWords, which includes ads in search results, is the primary vehicle used with Google.

- YouTube, the world's largest online video community, is owned by Google; advertising space is available and continuously added as videos are uploaded hourly by amateur and professional videographers from all over the world.

- Google Content Network, the world's largest online ad network, allows you to target relevant Web sites with text, banner, audio, and video advertising.

- DoubleClick™, an advertising management option offered by Google, provides resources for marketers, agencies, networks, and Web publishers to maximize and manage their Google ads and promotions.

- Google also offers a number of free tools for promoting your product or service and helps you optimize your likelihood to be discovered during Web searches.

- Google TV Ads walks you through the steps of creating, targeting, bidding, and optimizing television campaigns.

- Mobile ads reach customers who use and browse the Web through a mobile phone.

The options can be mind-boggling, and we will discuss all of these tools as they relate to your AdWords campaign so that you fully understand the resources available to you and your organization through the Google promotions powerhouse. The more you understand the way AdWords works, the more you understand the underlying principles that guide all of Google's promotional opportunities. You'll also learn how to determine which options will be most effective for you and how to develop a plan to get the most out of your investment.

Putting the pieces of the process together

With AdWords, the possibilities may seem endless, and they will be explored in depth later in the book. To fully understand what is possible with AdWords, you need to understand its basic terminology and concepts, plus the process you will go through as a Google advertiser.

The diagram at right gives you a simplified view of the way the process works. As it illustrates, before you begin the AdWords process, you should look at your status, get your AdWords account set up, and then implement your AdWords plan so that your ads appear on the Web. This is a simplified view of the process; we will examine the options and steps needed for you to make your AdWords plan

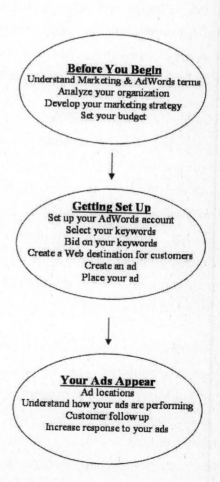

Before You Begin
Understand Marketing & AdWords terms
Analyze your organization
Develop your marketing strategy
Set your budget

Getting Set Up
Set up your AdWords account
Select your keywords
Bid on your keywords
Create a Web destination for customers
Create an ad
Place your ad

Your Ads Appear
Ad locations
Understand how your ads are performing
Customer follow up
Increase response to your ads

a reality more closely. To help you understand the full scope of this project, the diagram is divided in the same way that the sections of this book are divided.

The Google AdWords Philosophy

Google makes it clear throughout its AdWords site, as well as in its public corporate communications, that its primary business purpose is to provide the ultimate Internet search engine. The company maintains the integrity of the AdWords program based on this primary business purpose, and understanding this will help you understand many things about how to maximize all of Google's business solutions, including the AdWords program. Google explains this as its "effort to deliver increasingly relevant, compelling, and useful content to our users."

Google subscribes to the "less is more" philosophy, which makes for cleaner viewing of search results; non-invasive, attention-seeking gimmicks in its advertising; concise ads; and easy targeting. This philosophy also figures into the simplicity of design for the sign-up process and for accessing your AdWords account information. Einstein's famous mathematical equation, $E = mc^2$, looks simple, but there is a lot of thought behind it that resulted in its appearance of simplicity. Likewise, AdWords is simple to use, but can offer complex business information to you if you understand the complexity behind it.

Relevance is a concept that will be discussed in this book as it relates to your keywords, ads, landing pages, and everything else you may include on any of Google's online properties. If you can use relevance and usefulness as the touchstones for everything you do within Google's Business Solutions, your ad placement and search engine results will drastically improve, because this is what Google is looking for as they assign quality scores, boost your placement, and lower your cost. To read Google's AdWords philosophy in its entirety, go to **http://adwords.google.com/support/aw/bin/answer.py?hl=en&answer=45968&rd=1.**

Advertising and content policies

When you agree to the terms and conditions of Google's advertising programs, you agree to adhere to their policies regarding content. These are subject to change, so when in doubt, check the guidelines they have listed at **http://adwords.google.com/support/aw/bin/static.py?hl=en&page=guide_toc.cs&path=policy** before developing, writing, and launching a campaign that will be disapproved.

Here is a list of the things you may not promote through Google:

- anabolic steroids
- academic aids
- aids to pass drug tests
- alcohol
- bulk marketing
- copyrighted content
- violence

The first step in using Google AdWords is to gain a surface understanding of how the process works. Now that you understand the system's methodology, you can make AdWords work more effectively for you with the information in the following chapters.

Chapter Two

What Do I Need to Know to Make This Work for Me?

In every business, government, and nonprofit sector, there are acronyms galore and a language that is seemingly spoken only by those who are native to the processes, procedures, and nuances contained within its inner workings. The world of advertising and marketing is no different. Knowing and understanding advertising, marketing, and AdWords terms, and what they mean are fundamental to developing and implementing a strategy that works best.

In this chapter, you will learn keywords and concepts that will help you understand AdWords terms within the context of the marketing world in general, and how AdWords fits into the environment of Web marketing. This will broaden your understanding of why it works the way it does, and how you can most effectively use its components to positively impact your communications efforts. This chapter will start with some basic concepts that apply to the huge, broad scope of the marketing world and zoom in to focus on how these basics apply to Internet marketing and to AdWords.

This chapter is also our first opportunity to use our imaginary company — Hotcakes Emporium, which is exploring the possibility of selling its hotcakes online. Let us look at the basics of these terms — how they will apply to an online hotcakes business that is using AdWords as a primary means of advertising — and illuminate the practical application of these terms and concepts in the real world.

Please note that this chapter is intended as an overview or primer of the basics that will be discussed further in later chapters. To make this book as handy a reference as possible, you will find the basic versions of the definitions of new terms in boxes worked into and around the normal chapter text.

Ideas from World of Advertising and Marketing

The idea of exchanging goods and services for money, or by bartering, may have begun as far back as with the guy who learned how to harness fire and, perhaps, by his cave-neighbor, the wheel-inventor. Once each of these guys and their clans realized that they had something of value, they may have used them against rival clans, or exchanged them to get tools from friendly neighboring clans. Exchange for survival and for a better way of life seems to be an integral part of how we humans function on this planet.

Return on Investment (ROI)

As this concept of exchange has evolved, it has included the idea of fair exchange and competition. The idea of fair exchange is a simple one. It would be foolish to give you a state-of-the-art wheel to make your work go faster and easier in exchange for something as common and useless such as, say, a blade of grass. This is an example of a negative return on investment for the commerce wizard offering the wheel. Creating a valuable wheel would take brainpower, time, and energy. To get the proper return or payback from an exchange involving a wheel, its maker would expect something of equal or greater value.

Return on Investment (ROI). The amount, or ratio, you gain from the amount you put in.

As shown in this example, Return on Investment, or ROI, is important in every business venture and should be a gauge for understanding the effectiveness of any advertising, marketing, or public relations campaign. To determine this, subtract the cost of investment from the gain of investment, and divide by the cost of the investment. This calculation is commonly used to analyze marketing and advertising efforts through tracking campaigns and can be determined using both simple and complex factors.

The effectiveness of marketing strategy is determined by the ROI — return you get on your advertising, marketing, or public relations investment. If you traditionally run an ad in the local high school newspaper including a coupon or other promotional code in your ad, it is an easy way to determine how many high school students, parents, and faculty respond to your ad. This is campaign tracking. The next step in determining your ROI is to compare the number of coupons you received, or sales that were generated from the ad, with the amount that you paid for the ad. For example, if the ad cost $100, and you sold $150 of goods or services based on coupons redeemed, the ad paid for itself, and you had a positive return on your investment. This is a simplified version of how to calculate ROI:

(Gain of investment - Cost of investment) ÷ by Cost of investment + ROI

An enormous number of factors contribute to your ROI, including not only the cost for the advertising itself, but also:

- the cost (in terms of time) it took to create, approve, and place the ad

- the cost of any discounts or samples you offered

- the cost of training to prepare employees to handle customers that respond to the advertising

- the cost of additional goods or services needed to meet the advertising's promises

- the cost of fulfillment for shipping products

- the cost of additional labor to respond to customers

Look at an ROI example for our fictitious Hotcakes Emporium company.

If Hotcakes Emporium (HE) wants to analyze the ROI of a print ad in the local newspaper, the simple way to do this is to subtract the amount it paid for the ad ($300) from the amount of money received from the ten orders placed as a direct response to the ad ($420), and then to divide that number by the cost ($300).

The calculation would look like this:

$420 – $300 = $120
$120 divided by $300 = 0.4, or 40 percent

The Emporium's owner comes up with a 40 percent ROI using this simple calculation.

Using a more comprehensive business method, the following would also be included in the calculation with ten baskets sold in this scenario.

The retail price of gift baskets sold ($42 x 10 baskets = $420 made from the ad), minus the cost of baskets sold ($16 x 10 baskets = $160 labor and materials), equals the profit on each basket sold ($26 x 10 baskets = $260 profit).

Including these figures makes the ROI calculation look more like this:

$420 (orders placed)
-$160 (cost of baskets sold)
-$300 (cost for ad) = -$40
-$40 divided by $300 = -0.13, or -13%

In this example, the ad has a negative return on investment. To properly analyze the ROI, you must include other cost factors, such as overhead and the time it took to develop and proof the ad. You also must consider long-term benefits, such as obtaining the e-mail addresses of ten new customers for your e-mail newsletter distribution list, and the value of the ad's exposure to potential customers who did not order in direct response to the ad, but are now aware that HE products are available and may order in the future.

With AdWords, as with other business opportunities, you should consider both long-term and short-term investment returns. Information campaigns, which focus on gathering sales leads and building customer databases, typically would be considered long-term investment campaigns. An example of this would be an investment where you purchase real estate and plan to get your financial return from rental or depreciation values over time.

A short-term AdWords campaign would typically focus on making sales immediately from your landing page. An offline example of this would be purchasing a case of energy drinks at wholesale price and selling the drinks at an outdoor event the next weekend. In the latter case, you immediately collected the money you put into the drinks and made a profit.

A long-term AdWords campaign would include one that focuses on generating leads or information. Collecting these leads for a list of volunteers or donors for a charity, or compiling names and e-mail addresses for an e-mail marketing newsletter are examples of long-term AdWords campaign possibilities.

Target audience

An important factor in gaining the maximum ROI in your marketing efforts, and specifically, your AdWords ads and campaigns, is knowing your target audience. Your target is the group of people you are trying to reach. It is important to think of targets as specifically as possible. For example, the majority of businesses target potential customers. "Potential customers" can be separated by more specific terms such as:

- those who purchased your product from a competitor
- those who live within driving range of your store
- those who may not know you are in business
- those who have done business with you before, but have not become repeat customers
- those who are not aware that your pricing is highly competitive

You get the idea. Your target can be divided into segments by interest, geography, different products or services, or various status categories. AdWords makes it easy to write ads to target each potential audience you may have.

Target Audience. Those most likely to respond to, or benefit from, what you offer.

Some of Hotcake Emporium's targets would include:

- corporate gift basket purchasers

- personal gift basket purchasers

- people looking for an easy, inexpensive breakfast option for kids, family groups, and overnight guests

- civic organizations, schools, and churches that could use the hot-cakes as a fund-raising item

- bed and breakfast owners who could use something different on their menu

- specialty and gift shop owners that might sell gourmet food items in their stores

Public relations professionals may refer to a target audience as a "public" and multiple audiences referred to as "publics." This term can be interchangeable with the term "target audience," because a public is a group that is somehow connected by an interest or other factor. Publics are further classified by their relationship to an organization. Publics may be internal, such as employees, members, and investors; or external, such as distributors, government agencies, the media, community leaders, and consumers.

To make the most effective use of your communications investments, through AdWords and any other medium you may choose, you must recognize what public(s) you are trying to reach with your message and customize your message to appeal to that target.

Campaign

Campaign. A way of organizing and categorizing advertisements and marketing messages.

A campaign in the online universe is similar to an advertising, marketing, or public relations campaign in the offline world. Campaigns are set up in both of these environments to help keep your promotional efforts organized and typically revolve around a common goal, theme, season, product launch, piece of information, target audience, promotion, or offer. A campaign may consist of one or several ads and can run over varying time frames. An example of a long-running campaign is the "Eat Mor Chikin®" cow campaign that has been run by the fast food chicken restaurant Chick-fil-A® since 1995. This campaign features black and white cows that appear in ads encouraging fast food chicken consumption rather than eating hamburgers made of beef. *This is also a great example of branding, as explained in Chapter 4.*

When AdWords refers to a campaign, the category encompasses ad groups, which includes various ads. The following visual shows the hierarchy of ads, and the way you can sort them with AdWords. Note that a campaign does not have to include multiple ads, although that is more typical.

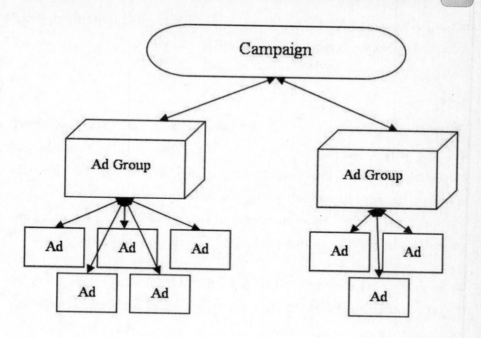

When you log into your AdWords account, you will go the Campaigns tab to manage your ads and campaigns. *This will be discussed more in-depth in Chapter 6.*

Ideas from the World of Web Marketing

Like the worlds of traditional advertising and marketing, Web, or Internet, marketing has a set of terms and concepts that are frequently used to describe commonly used actions, motives, and results. We could fill an entire book with these terms. Instead, we are going to focus on those that you need to understand, so that you can gain a more complete understanding of AdWords. Many of these terms have specific meanings to AdWords, and we will cover those here. *In the next section, we will look at AdWords' specific terms.* Meanwhile, glance over these explanations to give yourself a foundational understanding, and then come back to review them once you delve deeper into the AdWords process. These terms are in order, with the most basic concept appearing first, and the others ideas building on that one. Check out the boxes for basic definitions as you go.

Click

When Windows® computers were introduced to the marketplace, the first skill the tutorial taught was the action of clicking with the mouse. That mouse click denotes a selection of text, an image, a hyperlink, or some other object that appears on the computer screen. The click is also now used to transport the "clicker" of an AdWords ad to a website that is set up by the advertiser. AdWords measures clicks, which measures interest in your ad.

Users must select your ad with their mouse or their cursor, then click on the ad to get to your website. The number of times that users actually do this is referred to as your number of clicks. This translates as: Those who are interested enough in your ad to get more information are those who click on it. Using Hotcakes Emporium as an example, this is how it works:

1. Someone does a Google search for "breakfast food ideas" and sees several ads on the right side of the search page under "Sponsored Links."

2. One of these ads is the Hotcakes Emporium ad, which interests the person doing the search. In order to find out more information about hotcakes delivery, the person selects the ad and then clicks on it.

3. They go to the Hotcakes Emporium site.

4. Hotcakes Emporium pays Google for bringing a visitor to the site via the AdWords ad.

Note that Hotcakes Emporium has not sold anything or gotten information from this interested "clicker." They are paying Google for the opportunity to sell to, or otherwise engage, the person that clicks on their ad, which Google allowed to appear in its search results.

Cost-per-click (CPC)

Every time a Google user clicks on one of your ads, if you are using cost-per-click, or CPC, that means that you pay Google. CPC is one of the two ways that Google charges you for advertising (cost-per-thousand impressions — CPM is the other. See following definition.). These are both typical measures of online advertising. It is important to note that when Google says "pay only for results" that you are not paying for every sale, or for every person that signs up for your newsletter, or for every e-mail address that you get to add to your database. You are paying if they click on your ad. With AdWords, you bid in a CPC auction to determine how much you will pay for every click. The minimum CPC is $.01. Even though you bid on your CPC, it can be lower if your AdWords quality score improves. *Refer to the discussion of quality score in Chapter 8. This topic is also further discussed under the "Bidding" topic in Chapter 6.*

Impressions

Impressions are the number of times your ad appears to a Google user. For example, if your ad for home delivery of your new blueberry-flavored hotcake mix has 1,000 impressions, it has been shown 1,000 times as a result of a Google search. This information will be displayed in the AdWords reporting statistics as "Impr." When your ad appears, or makes an impression, interested Google users click on it to go to your website, so a click is involved even when you are focused on impressions. You can pay per impressions or per clicks. But, even if you pay-per-click, you still want to know how many times your ad appears as a result of a Google search, which is its number of impressions. This number is important to let you know how many times it appears versus how many times it is clicked on, which can give you an idea of how attractive your ad is to those it appears to.

Cost-per-thousand impressions (CPM)

CPM is one of the two ways that Google charges you for advertising. Cost-per-click is the other, as previously explained. With AdWords, if you are using CPM pricing, you pay Google for every 1,000 impressions, or for every 1,000 times that your ad appears on a page. With these two options, you choose if you prefer to pay when someone sees your ad (CPM), or when someone takes action in response to your ad (CPC). It is also important to note that with AdWords, CPM is available only for use on campaigns that include "placements," which means that you specify that you want your ads placed, or appearing, on certain sites. This controls the impressions or appearances of your ads and limits them to appear only on those sites that you specify. Of course, you should that specify target sites be closely connected and viewed by your target audience. The goal here is to limit your audience and increase the cost effectiveness of your ad.

Click-through rates (CTR)

Your click-through rates, or CTR, let you know the percentage of people that see your ad as compared to the number of people that see it and click on it. The CTR for a keyword lets you know how relevant it is to users, because it shows how successfully that keyword persuades interested users to select your ad. CTR is determined by a simple formula. Divide the number of clicks by the number of impressions, or times that your ad is shown to a user. For example if your ad has 1,000 impressions, or is shown 1,000 times, and people click on your ad 100 times, your CTR is 10 percent.

With AdWords, the high CTR also makes your quality score higher, which gives you a higher ad position and lower costs for your ad. This principle applies to both ads and keywords. This helps you determine which ads are more effective than others, and, likewise, which keywords bring you the best results. The reverse is also true. If an ad's CTR is low, that ad is not performing well. If a keyword's CTR is low, AdWords recommends that you consider ad or keyword optimization, or more effectively including your keywords in your ad.

1,000 impressions ÷ 100 clicks = 10% CTR

For example, Hotcakes Emporium runs an ad for its Hotcakes Sampler Gift Basket that appears as the result of the keyword phrases "breakfast food ideas" and "breakfast food gifts." The CTR for breakfast food ideas is lower than that for breakfast food gifts. This may be because people searching for ideas are probably looking for recipes, and those looking for gifts are more likely to be interested in ordering a gift basket, therefore, clicking on the ad for it, and making a purchase.

Conversion rates

Understanding the term "conversion rate" means understanding the statistic that is vital to determining the success, or failure, of any promotional efforts that you make online. It is calculated by determining the percentage of visitors who take the action that you want them to take, whether it be placing an order, registering for your e-mail newsletter, completing a questionnaire, or requesting more information. Hotcakes Emporium has found that its conversion rates are higher for certain keywords and focuses its efforts on those keywords that actually result in a gift basket order, rather than a visitor just browsing the site to see if it is true that hotcakes can be delivered to their door.

Conversion tracking

Conversion tracking is a way of tracking your conversion rates, or desired results. It is also the name of a free AdWords tool that allows you to measure results from your ads. Sign up, sales, or leads that your ads generate on your site determine the results. If a Google user clicks on your ad and looks at your landing page, this is not considered a conversion. If a user clicks on your ad and places an order, or fills in the information you request, that is considered a conversion. In both of these cases, you, as the advertiser, are paying for the users who click on your ad. In the first example, the click that you paid for does not gain you a return on your investment because you get nothing for the click you paid for. In the second example, the user responded to your ad by clicking on it and did what you wanted them to do. This second user "converted" from a clicker / browser to a positive return on your click investment.

Optimization

Optimization is used to get the maximum exposure for your online content, whether it is for ads, website, blog, or other Web content. This is often shown as SEO, or Search Engine Optimization, and summarizes the mind-set of the current climate in Internet promotions of every kind. It is accomplished by including the most relevant, most searched keywords within the content so that your ad, website, blog, or content appears as a result of a Web search. This may involve changing your keyword settings, adding new keywords, and improving the text of your contents and ads.

For example, the owner of Hotcakes Emporium writes some articles for small business publications and posts them on Emporium's website. Frequently used keywords and keyword phrases are woven throughout the content of these articles, which makes the site more likely to appear as a result of those keyword searches; Emporium receives greater visibility and a greater chance of promoting its products. To optimize its AdWords ads, the Emporium uses keywords as part of the headline or text.

As you work to optimize your ads and your online presence, keep in mind that Google uses technology to determine the quality of its searches, which is based on relevance and quality rather than simply if the keyword or phrase appears. The message here from Google is: Create content for your users, do not just stuff your content with keywords; include keywords in content that are applicable to the search.

Within the help section of AdWords, you will find an entire section called the Google AdWords Optimization Center devoted to optimization. Within this area, you may view tips by your level of expertise, for each account feature, or by advertising goal. To access this, search for Optimization Center in the Search Help box at the top of the AdWords help section or go to: **http://adwords.google.com/support/aw/bin/static. py?hl=en&guide=21804&page=guide.cs.**

Basic AdWords Terms to Understand and Implement

The language and process of AdWords is not complicated. The names of tools and concepts typically describe their function, which makes it much easier for the beginner, the seasoned professional, and everyone in between to navigate through the AdWords system. The terms here are offered as an overview to give you a basic understanding of what it is, what it does, and how you use it. Most, if not all, of the terms, concepts, and flow of AdWords will be discussed more in-depth in other chapters as they apply to your needs as an advertiser. Please note that AdWords is continually evolving and, as of this writing, these terms and their definitions are up-to-date.

Keywords

Keywords are especially important to understand. They drive when and where your ads appear, so that users can click on them. Every time a Google search user enters one of your keywords in a Google search query, your ad could appear in the area beside the search results under "Sponsored Links." For example, if you are offering your hotcake mix as part of a corporate gift basket and use "corporate food gifts" as a keyword, your ad may show on the "corporate food gifts" results page. Finding keywords to use at the onset of your AdWords experience is easy. *AdWords offers free tools for this, which will be discussed in Chapter 7.* The thing to understand about keywords is that all of your keywords are not worth including, because the response to them will be low. Likewise, the most popular keywords all of your competitors might be using might not get enough results to merit paying for them. The ROI of your keywords must be considered if you want to keep maintaining your budget, and your results, from your AdWords campaigns.

Some low-response keywords for Hotcakes Emporium might include:

- **Pancakes.** This is a broad topic for another name for hotcakes, which is used regionally in the South. Is the search for recipes, mixes, or the history of pancakes?

- **Hotcakes recipe.** This keyword search results in recipes for those who want to make hotcakes themselves, not purchase a mix.

- **Hotcakes image.** Those searching for an image to use, rather than a mix to purchase, would likely use this keyword.

Landing page

When a customer clicks on an AdWords ad, that click takes them to a landing page. This page can be the home page to your website or a page uniquely designed to showcase a special offer or sign-up incentive. When you fill in the text for your AdWords ad, there is a spot for you to put a destination URL and a display URL. The destination URL is invisible to viewers of your ad, but it drives those who click on your ad to your landing page. The display URL is usually the website address that you want users to see, so you can direct clickers to different pages within your site as they respond to different ads you have appearing on AdWords. *For more about landing pages, see Chapter 7*

Placements

A placements is a term that AdWords uses to describe where an ad will be placed within its content or advertising network. With placements, ads appear on specific Web pages, rather than beside search results. As with much of Google's advertising and business solutions, with placements, you have options. These options include automatic, managed, and excluded. Text ads appear in response to a Google search. Ads with placements appear when a Google user goes to a specific website. *Read more about Content*

Network information in Chapter 5. Meanwhile, the basics of what you need to know about placing your ad on Google's vast array of website and other content partners, is that you can let Google select where your ads appear, or you can select where your ads appear. *Set your preferred placements under the Campaign tab of your AdWords account; this will be covered in detail in Chapter 6.*

Automatic placements.

Using the automatic placements options gives Google the go-ahead to search your ads for keywords and other cues and place your ads on pages within its Content Network that offer content relevant to your ad.

Managed

If you would like to manage your own ad placements, rather than have Google do this for you, you can opt for more control through managed placements.

Excluded

If there is a website, a category of sites, or a type of Web page that you do not want to show your ad, you can exclude them from your list of placements.

Quiz: Do I Understand the Google AdWords Lingo?

1. What are the two ways you can pay for your AdWords ads?

2. What action takes Google users to your landing page?

3. What measurement lets you know how many times Google users click on your ad as compared to how many times your ad appeared?

4. What is the measurement of how much you receive compared to how much you invest?

5. What is the Google system for creating, placing, and measuring ads that appear within Google's properties?

6. What is the term that describes how many times your ad appears?

7. What are the three types of ad placements options?

8. What term describes placements that Google does for you?

9. If you do not want your ad to show on a website, Web page, or category of websites, what type of placements do you select?

10. If you want to control the placements of your ads yourself, what type of placements do you choose?

11. What term describes those you are trying to reach who might be most interested in what your ads offer?

12. What do you do to make your AdWords ads and campaigns as effective as possible?

13. What is a grouping of ads that have a target audience, product, special event, or time frame in common called?

14. What term describes paying for every 1,000 times your ad appears?

15. What term describes paying for every time a Google user clicks on your ad and goes to your landing page?

16. What is the name of the trigger that Google users search for that you can connect to your ad's appearance?

17. How do you determine how many "clickers" just visited your website versus how many "clickers" completed the desired reaction when they reached your website?

18. What number is vital to understanding the success of your online promotional efforts?

Answers

1. Cost-per-click (CPC) and Cost-per-thousand impressions (CPM)
2. Clicking on your ad
3. Click-through rates (CTR)
4. Return on investment (ROI)
5. AdWords
6. Impressions
7. Automatic, managed, and excluded
8. Automatic
9. Excluded
10. Managed
11. Target audience
12. Optimization
13. A campaign
14. Cost-per-thousand impressions (CPM)
15. Cost-per-click (CPC)
16. Keywords
17. Conversion tracking
18. Conversion rates

Chapter Three

What Do I Need to Know About My Business to Get Started?

As a small business owner, and former employee of several small- to mid-sized businesses, I understand that the daily activities of a business or organization can easily sweep you into a mode where customer and employee demands monopolize your time. When you are in that state, there is not a lot of time or energy for planning and management.

It is important to take some time periodically to look at your business and compare what you want to be doing with what you actually are doing. The result of this examination should be your mission statement, and from that, you can set your goals and objectives. To ensure your organization's success, you need a plan.

Defining Your Mission

At this point, you may decide to skip to the chapter about how to set up your AdWords account; however, understand that a huge component of Google AdWords' effectiveness is the ability to easily analyze how your ads and campaigns are doing. When you set up your ads and campaigns based on your stated goals and objectives, you can easily and actively compare the numbers and determine how to use the AdWords program most effectively to move your company forward and accomplish your mission.

HOT TIP: A mission statement should be a concise summary of your organization's purpose and philosophy.

Goals and objectives for your organization

Businesses at any stage can use goals and objectives. Businesses in the formative or testing stage should view goals and objectives as an integral part of their business plan. Financial institutions and investors are more likely to support an organization with a comprehensive strategy to reach profitability. Established businesses can use the thought process that goes into setting goals and objectives as a method of determining whether business processes, functions, and departments are supporting the mission statement. Use your goals and objectives to measure current effectiveness, then add to them, or change them to effect organizational change that supports the mission.

A mission statement captures your organization's purpose, customer orientation, and business philosophy. It should be as concise as possible. In three sentences or less, explain what you are doing, and why you are doing it. For example, if you are a small, family business that is working to provide the best service and products in your industry, say so. If you are a nonprofit organization that began in order to provide transportation to doctor's appointments for the elderly, your mission statement should include why this service is important. Is it to make you feel good? Is it to bring more business to the doctors? Is it to improve the quality of life for these patients? Whatever it is, say it.

A clear, concise mission statement can motivate you and those who encounter your business or organization. Employees who support your mission statement and share the company vision can more effectively help you achieve your measurable goals and objectives. Your mission statement can also help you determine target audiences and keywords in your Google AdWords campaigns. It should give you some guidance about your potential customers, as well as words and phrases you use to describe your products and services that will help you create your keyword list, and, therefore, match your products and services with those who are most likely to be interested in purchasing them.

Once you have your mission statement, set specific goals and objectives. These can keep you focused and help you move forward in the direction that you want to be going. Write them down. Make a poster. Send e-mail. Do not let the opportunity to capture this important information pass you by without acting on it. Seasoned business professionals, as well as inexperienced entrepreneurs, can be sidetracked.

Businesses of any size or level of maturity regularly map their strategies to ensure that employees in every department, even management and shareholders, are working to achieve the same result. Specific, measurable goals and objectives are important components in an effective business plan and are necessary in an effective marketing plan. It is also important to remember that goals and objectives change. They should have some flexibility because the marketplace is flexible, just like many other factors affecting your business.

Goals and objectives work together, but they are not the same. Goals are more general, while objectives are specific ways to reach the goals. Both should be measurable. If you have a number included in your goal or objective, such as a date, a dollar amount, a mile radius, or a percentage, you are probably on the right track. Both should use what you know about your business, your competition, the marketplace, available resources, suppliers, customers, and all other factors that affect what you do.

HOT TIP: Goals and objectives must be measurable.

For example, a goal of most businesses is to make more money. This goal, however, is obvious and does not really give much insight into what should be happening with your business. Instead of "make more money," determine your objectives by asking a couple of questions:

1. How do we make more money? This question is the basis of your marketing strategy. For now, break this down into some preliminary answers to other questions, such as: "How have we made money in the past?" and "How are we making money now?" Be prepared to look at your current revenue streams and broaden your scope of ways to add revenue to your current business.

2. How much more money do we want to make? Narrow that down. Do you want to make $1 more, or $100,000 more? Do you want to make enough money to buy equipment, build infrastructure, or upgrade software? You get the idea — decide what you want specifically. Set a number. Charitable organizations and church building funds frequently use a giant thermometer graph to give some visual impact and relevance to how much money a fund-raiser is bringing in, or how many new members they may have. Think in terms of the giant picture of a thermometer graph that can be filled in as results come in, and you come closer to meeting your goal.

So, if the answer to the question of how to make more money is to get more customers, continue to follow this train of thought to determine how many more customers you need, how many customers must be repeat customers, and how you are going to get these customers. Make your objectives specific so you can measure your progress. This allows you to see if what you are doing to get more customers, your objective, is really helping you meet your goal of making more money.

One way to visualize the goals of your organization is to see them as the backbone or the skeletal structure that holds your business together, establishes your form, and directs your movement. Because AdWords offers the possibility for you to move toward different audiences, you can do this more effectively if you set your goals first.

If goals are the skeletal structure, then specific, measurable objectives are the muscle that moves your business in its annual, quarterly, monthly, weekly, and daily activities. Every customer you gain moves you closer to meeting this objective, which works with other objectives to meet the goals of your business or organization.

AdWords and your business goals

So, what do your organization's goals and objectives have to do with Google AdWords? AdWords helps you meet a number of your organization's goals and objectives — or just one of your choosing. Although AdWords allows for increased revenue and for testing new products, it can also help you do other things, such as develop a human resources component to your business. There are job seekers who use the Web to find jobs locally, or who may be interested in relocating for a job with your company. Freelance professionals are also searching the Web for new clients. Highly specialized expertise is often more affordable for short-term projects when you use freelance professionals who may live outside of commuting distance to your office. AdWords is a great way to start looking for these types of future employees.

Plan your business activities based on the measurable objectives that reflect your goals. Use them to make important business decisions. If an opportunity that sounds great initially does not match with your businesses goals, you may want to think seriously about skipping the opportunity or reevaluating your goals. Remember to be flexible with your goals and objectives. Change them to adjust to changes in the marketplace, which may include:

- changes in the number of competitors battling for the same customers.

- changes relating to your suppliers, which could come in the form of cost and availability of equipment. An example of this would be shipping and transportation costs, which can affect Web-based business transactions involving products. Your cost to ship your products to your customers directly impacts your bottom line. If shipping costs rise, an AdWords ad offering free shipping might bring you more customers by giving you an edge over your competitor.

The worksheet at the end of this chapter will help you set goals and analyze your business, so that you can most effectively run your business and use AdWords as a medium to further your unique goals. Once you analyze your business, you can use the analytical tools in Google AdWords to determine if an ad or campaign will benefit your business. If it does not, you can easily make changes until it does.

Analyze your business

Establishing measurable goals does not always have to be your first step. New or unestablished businesses should start with the goals and objectives section, while businesses that have been around for a while should analyze where they are currently. These businesses will then establish their goals and objectives based on existing factors. For example, once you analyze your marketing plan and realize that you really do not have a plan that can be implemented and then measured, you can set your goals or objectives accordingly. Or, you can use marketing information from past campaigns and use it to set new goals or objectives, depending on what was and was not successful.

Armed with your mission statement and your measurable goals and objectives, you can look at each of the components in this section and effect some positive change in your organization. Be patient with yourself if you are making changes in the thoughts and direction that you are going. As the saying goes, a big ship turns slowly, and the bigger the ship, your business or organization, the slower it turns. With that said, consider taking baby steps toward change as you analyze where you are and compare that with where you would like to be.

What Do You Really Do?

What sells the most may not make you the most money. So, look at what you do and how to incorporate that into your goals and objectives, therefore, into your marketing plan for increased profitability using AdWords. As you move through this section, be prepared to look at your sales results from the past. If you are a new business or organization, relate the information in this section to your perceptions of which of your products or services will be the most popular. Retail products are easier to compare, but if yours is a service organization, think of each of your services as a single product. Even though it may be something you do for customers rather than a physical item that you give to them, think of each of your services as being wrapped in a gift box, so you can more easily conceptualize each item.

Selling a product

Retail establishments typically offer a variety of products for consumers. Options can sometimes give you more of a chance to be the provider of the product. Consumers like options, which is why phrases like "Largest Selection" and "Top Name Brands" are often included in advertisements. These phrases let the potential customer know that you are able to meet their needs, no matter how specific they may be.

As you analyze your business, it is important to look at what drives your profitability. Often, retailers use a "bait" item to draw customers to them, hopefully leading to the customer picking up another item or two, or five, or ten. They may not make a lot of money on the advertised item, but the additional money made via the additional store traffic makes advertising the lesser item worthwhile. For example, consumers may respond to an advertisement for a sale on paper towels. While they are in the store buying the paper towels, they will hopefully remember they also need toothpaste, bread, and vitamins. In this case, the paper towels are the top seller, but they are not the top moneymaker. The top moneymaking product, or the product that gives you, the retailer, the most profitability, may be the easiest to produce or cost the least. It may be the most profitable because people are willing to pay more for it, because it is either scarce or popular.

For example, a stay-at-home mother, Kim, is a talented seamstress and sews in her spare time. Kim has a small business making appliquéd T-shirts, bags, aprons, and children's clothing, and can put a monogram on just about anything. She also makes and sells hair bows. To sell her accessories, she often gets a booth at a crafts fair or flea market. It is not the hair bows that draw women to her booth — but it is the hair bows that they buy overwhelmingly. Apparently, having a hair bow to match every outfit keeps them coming back for more. And, while shoppers peruse the huge variety of colors and styles of bows, they may pick up a T-shirt, a bag, an apron, or an outfit to match the new bow.

In Kim's case, the bows are the least expensive for her to make because her supplies, the ribbon and the clip used to attach the bow, are inexpensive. She can also make a large number of these quickly. The bags take more time to make, and the material for them is more expensive than the material for the bows, so she charges more for them, but her profit margin on the bows is greater than it is on the bags. She must sell two bows to make the same amount of profit she makes on selling one bag.

Now that she has measured the profitability of her current products, she can set measurable goals for each of them of how many she would like to sell. She can then divide those goals into measurable objectives of how she would like to sell them. An example would be to set her sales goal for each craft fair at $200. She can then determine how many of each of her bows, bags, and other monogrammed items she must sell to make $200. Using her past sales information, she knows that she will probably sell five bows to every bag she sells. She sells the bows for about $5. The bags are $10. If she sells 30 bows at $5 each, and six bags at $10 each, she will make $210 and reach her goal. So, her measurable objectives to reach this goal would be to sell 30 bows and six bags.

The craft fair booths work great for her. To expand her business and sell these products on AdWords most effectively, she could easily develop an ad campaign using hair bows as the draw to her website, because they are the most sold item, then showcase her bags and other customizable products, just as she does at the crafts fairs. She could do this by featuring hair bows in an ad, and then, once the ads drive potential customers to her website, she could offer a discount on her bags and other customizable products. Another idea is to offer free shipping with purchases over a certain amount.

This will help her offset her costs of shipping one hair bow, as opposed to several products in the same order.

Promoting a service

Service businesses are unlike products businesses because there is not a tangible "thing" that can be looked at on the shelf and compared to similar things. Service businesses are called that for a reason — although they may sell products as part of what they do, such as maid services selling cleaning supplies, their primary purpose is to provide a service rather than a product.

In analyzing your service business, it is important to determine what makes you the most money. A family-owned electronic security business in Alabama has grown over the past 12 years from zero subscribers to being ranked as one of the largest privately held companies of its kind in the state. The company has done this primarily by the word-of-mouth recommendations of its customers. It started out installing security systems in homes and small businesses.

Why is this business considered a service business when it is selling electronic security components? In this case, the business's primary function is not to sell security system components. It is to provide the installation of these components. Then, once installed, systems are monitored by a central station that receives burglary, fire, health, and panic alarm signals and then dispatches the appropriate emergency response personnel. The primary purpose of this business is to install, monitor, and service electronic security devices, not to sell the devices themselves.

When this business started out, it offered free service for systems it installed. This is one of the things that gave this service business a boost in customers, but it served as a cash flow drain. Service customers would pay for equipment that needed to be replaced, but the cost of labor was absorbed by the business. In analyzing the business, the partners realized that even though this had been great for building the business at the beginning, once customers multiplied, service calls multiplied. Multiplied service calls, in turn, increased labor expense, which began to make an enormous financial strain on the business.

After analyzing competitors' service rates, and comparing service rates for different industries in their geographic area, the business set hourly rates just a little lower than their competitors, but high enough to cover labor cost and overhead with a small profit margin. Had this business not analyzed this component of its service, it probably would have closed, despite the fact that it was continuing to grow its customer base. Servicing any type of electronic security devices and systems is now a profitable revenue stream.

In the case of this service business, offering discounted service rates on existing security systems for homes through an AdWords campaign could make this area of the business even more profitable, and also help convert competitors' customers. This business could run simultaneous AdWords campaigns that use both service and product keywords. For example, it could use "security system monitoring" as a service keyword, and "wireless security system" as a product keyword. The monitoring it provides is a service, but because it services security products, it can also use the names of those products as keywords to attract customers to its services.

If you have a service business and are not selling associated products to your customers, explore doing so as an option to provide an additional revenue stream for your business. Consider posting an ad on AdWords offering a free or discounted product as an incentive for new customers to try your service.

Your mission versus your daily activities

Many nonprofits are started by one person who sees a need and is affected enough by that need to spend their time and energy to meet it. Although nonprofits are not functioning to make a profit, they, like any business, must have revenue to operate and to support their cause. The operations of many nonprofits include fund-raising and awareness so others can support their cause by donating time, talent, or money.

Fund-raising and volunteer recruitment and management can monopolize the time of a nonprofit. That is not a bad thing, as long as the funds raised are actually being used to support the cause and not simply to support more fund-raising. One way to avoid this is to create a mission statement and live by it.

For Our Country, Inc. (FOCI) is a nonprofit that was started to support other established nonprofit organizations that support veterans of the Armed Forces who have been wounded while serving our country. The ultimate mission for this organization is to give back to veterans. FOCI will do this by using music industry professionals, including songwriters, producers, and artists, to create music based on the letters, poetry, journal entries, songs, and thoughts of the veterans themselves.

This organization is a great example to follow because the core of the mission is to help wounded veterans. The mission's method is to help them by creating an album to create awareness. The creation of the album will consume most of the organization's efforts. In this case, that is perfect, because it dovetails with the mission statement and has the most probability for effecting change for wounded veterans. Collecting the veterans' submissions, making selections from them, writing songs, recording and producing the songs, then distributing the album through military organizations and music venues is an enormous undertaking and is the focus of the organization's efforts and daily activities.

What if the mission statement had focused on providing medical treatment to wounded veterans? Creating an album to fund this mission would still be a creative way to do that, but the organization's initial primary functions should be in making veterans aware of its services — obtaining medical supplies, and hiring professional medical staff and administrators to serve veterans' medical needs — rather than as a creative outlet to raise funds. Remember, the mission statement must be the reference point to ensure that your daily activities, as well as large-scale projects, are moving in the direction that the organization states that it wants to move.

Target Audience

Knowing your target audience is important with any advertising, marketing, or public relations campaign. With AdWords, knowing whom to target is especially important because your ads really show in front of Google users who are already seeking information about something that relates to what your business is trying to accomplish. In this section, learn ways to pinpoint your target audience and select keywords, which will help bring revenue and sales information into your business.

Your target is anyone who could be, or should be, connected to your organization. They are many types of target audiences, or publics, including internal and external. Internal publics often include employees because they are inside the organization. External publics are outside of the organization, but can somehow be affected by what the organization does. For example, potential customers are not currently part of the organization, but, of course, they should be. Everyone is not a potential customer. With an AdWords campaign, everyone who searches on the Internet is not a possibility for being affected by your organization. This means they will not affect your organization by exchanging information or money for your product or service. To understand who your target audience is, you must understand whom they are not. The nonprofit mentioned earlier, FOCI, can help demonstrate how to define targets.

Who does FOCI affect? Wounded veterans, but that is just the easy, surface answer. So, ask a question that requires a more definitive response. Putting the mission statement, or your measurable goals and objectivism, in the form of a question can be helpful.

Who does FOCI need to accomplish the mission of assisting wounded veterans through music in the form of an album? This is better; you now know this list will need to include volunteers, music industry professionals, and established nonprofits that already do this. To fund and begin the process of creating the album, FOCI first reaches out to potential donors to help fund the organization. The list now includes:

Its first-tier targets: organizations and individuals willing to sponsor the organization.

Its second-tier targets include:

- professional songwriters
- music producers
- recording artists
- wounded veterans
- established nonprofits that help wounded veterans
- other volunteers to help manage the project
- potential customers of the album

These are your basics, but a target has rings that surround the bull's-eye for a reason. Keep the image of a bull's-eye in mind as you further narrow whom to target for this example, so you can easily apply this thought process in determining your target audience and your AdWords keywords. When narrowing target audiences, it is helpful to scribble out a factor tree to help keep up with the divisions and not lose your train of thought. To do this, put your organization, product, or service at the top of the page. Then, list the targets that must get the message that you are trying to share. Keep narrowing the target list as much as you can until you cannot narrow the target any further. Once you get your factor tree drawn, you can select the targets and the best method of communicating with them. A partial factor tree for FOCI is shown next:

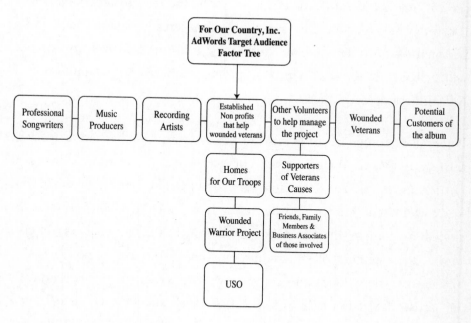

Would it be beneficial for all professional songwriters to be involved? No. That would be too many; so, narrow that down to target professional songwriters in Nashville, where FOCI is headquartered. This is still broad. We really want songwriters living in Nashville who will volunteer to write these songs using lyrics, thoughts, and feelings provided by the soldiers.

The next step is to find out about this group of people you are targeting. If you do not know much about your target audience, do a little research. The more you can learn to think like your target, the more effective all of your marketing and advertising will be. AdWords advertising is no exception.

Now, determine how to reach this target. A similar thought process to narrow the target would also apply to music producers and artists. In these cases, AdWords will probably not be the best venue to use to reach these targets because the list of targets is small and already defined. One of the great things about AdWords is that it can be used to create a database, or list, for your target. In this case, this list has already been created, and a personal call or letter to some studios, associations, and industry friends will probably do the trick here. But, pinpoint another target audience that AdWords can greatly affect.

Potential customers of the album are definitely a target that can be reached through AdWords. But this is still a broad target. Who would be interested in such an album? For starters, if you had a friend or family member who was a wounded veteran, and he or she had even the smallest phrase included in a song in this album, you would buy it. But, the soldiers will take care of that segment of your target by word-of-mouth, or possibly with online social networking themselves. As explained in the music producers and artists target example earlier, AdWords should be used to help you create a targeted list or database of those who will respond to the information, products, and services your organization is promoting. If you already have such a list, use other means, besides AdWords, to promote to that list. AdWords can be a powerful tool to promote your organization, and when you use it in conjunction with word-of-mouth, social networking, and other marketing venues, it becomes even more powerful. This organization is a great example of how you can use AdWords with other media to comprehensively reach all of your target markets. Look at how AdWords now comes into play with FOCI.

Patriotic Americans who love music would be interested in this album and in supporting this cause. That does not mean they would necessarily seek out patriotic-sounding music to listen to, however. So, if this target is not doing a Google search for this type of music specifically, how can we use AdWords to make them aware of this album and purchase it to help these veterans?

Your target is patriotic Americans who love music, so work on dividing this definition into manageable chunks. Patriotic Americans and lovers of music narrow it down a little more. Two categories will be easy to focus on through both AdWords and Google's Content Network. There are search options galore for music of different genres, and many of those genres will be included on the album. The well-known artists who record the songs on the album will each be a searchable topic. Also, patriotic Americans may do searches on news events, politics, American history, schools, and community information. On the Content Network (which uses keywords to target websites where your ad can appear), news sites, blogs, websites, and community forums should all be considered as potential venues for getting out the message of this worthy organization to create awareness, as well as to encourage supporters to donate and to purchase the album.

Current and past customers

Although it is important to focus on gaining new customers or targeting potential customers, do not forget to target your past and current customers. Their loyalty is valuable. They can provide consistent, repeat business without the same time and expense required to attract new customers. Why is this the case?

- Current customers are already aware of you. You do not have to conduct advertising, marketing, or public relations campaigns to move into their field of vision because you are already there.

- Current customers can help maintain your business. Service contracts and repeat business with current customers cost less than convincing a new customer to try your product or service for the first time.

- Current customers have already changed their behavior at least once to include you in their purchase or service decision, so it is actually easier for them to continue to do so.

Past customers chose your product or service at least once before, so it may be easier to get them to do so again. But, if they had a negative experience with your business through a faulty product or a disappointing level of service, they may be a little harder to get back into the current customer category. It is possible that they are not current customers because a competitor caught their eyes, or they may have just not needed your service again. It is also possible they just forgot about you. Because your business is what you do every day, it is an active part of your thought process. It is probably not at the forefront of the minds of most other people unless they have a current need that your business can fulfill.

Your AdWords ad can remind them of that need by appearing on the pages of search results that you know have worked for you in the past. If there is a keyword that gets results, keep using it. Humans are creatures of habit, and if someone searches for a certain type of vitamin once, they may do the same search when it is time to refill. In this case, if they ordered vitamin C from you, and do a search for vitamin C, they may recognize your company name from the label of their now-empty vitamin C bottle. If they searched for chewable, fruit-flavored vitamin C tablets, and you have used this phrase in your AdWords ad, they are likely to see your ad at the top of the search results, as well as recognize your company name in the AdWords ad. Brand recognition (*which will be discussed more in Chapter 4*) and product satisfaction are both now coming into play as this customer clicks on your ad and places an order.

Marketing to past and current customers is done well through direct means, such as e-mail and printed direct mail. In those situations, you already have a targeted list. One of the inherently positive things about AdWords is that your ad is placed where it is relevant. People are searching for it if they see your ad. Your information was at one time relevant to your current and past customers. If you are a women's clothing retailer, as you continue to target new customers through AdWords, it is likely that your current and past customers will also see your ad, which could trigger a reminder of what they previously purchased from you and bring them to your site to make an additional purchase. When you use AdWords to bring in new customers and to remind past customers that your products are available, follow up with e-mail and direct mail to these targets to keep them coming back. This way, they will remember your company name when they see your ad on AdWords.

Your current business status

"Current business status" is just like it sounds — it is the condition of every aspect of your business right now. This phrase is only three words, but there is an enormous amount of information that determines what is really going on with your business. To accurately assess the status of your business or organization, you must divide it into components, departments, and functions. For large companies with large numbers of employees, the divisions may need to be narrowed even more. Determining where you are in every aspect of your business will help you make needed changes or help cultivate what you are already doing to make your business successful. This is the same principle used in AdWords with the testing of keywords, ads, and campaigns. Knowing your status will also help you prioritize your marketing strategy.

Understanding the job functions throughout your organization can be of great benefit in accurately assessing your business status at any time. You may not be the one answering the phone, doing the marketing, or shipping your products, but if there is a problem in any area with any job function, it directly affects your business, because it affects your customers. If you understand that the function of being a technician means that sometimes arriving at a customer's home dirty after crawling under a house at the last stop is a likely possibility. Providing shoe covers to these technicians can keep customers happy, lower complaints, and prevent the technicians from having to apologize as soon as they walk in the door. This move seems like a small thing, but it can reduce calls to your call center from customers who complain about mud being tracked through their homes. It also makes technicians more comfortable handling the installation or repair in the customer's home the first time. It may eliminate repeat service calls for the same initial service, which can cost money. Ultimately it also will allow phone customer service personnel to help more customers with reduced hold time; more important, it keeps your customers happy and reinforces their decision to do business with you. It also reduces stress on your employees, which can prevent more illness and time off caused by stress and will help save your business money.

With this example in mind, look at everything within your business. Tweak, delete, upgrade, train, and, most important, listen. If you do not understand a job function, ask the employee who performs the function everyday. Employees often have valuable insights into what customers request and how the business can operate more efficiently. As you do all of this, keep in mind that as your business runs smoother, it is easier to take care of customers and do it well. You should anticipate increased business once you get going with AdWords. Looking at, and working on, different parts of your business will prepare you for growth and open up communication between departments and employees so you can handle an increase in your advertising, as well as an increase in your business.

Analyze every component of your business. Record the information you get by creating charts, graphs, lists, processes, and procedures. This is time consuming, but it will be worth your time and efforts when you can use it as a basis to set goals and objectives and keep your customers happy while getting an edge on your competition. Here is a brief list of areas to analyze in your status review:

- customer service
- human resources and training
- IT
- accounting
- accounts payable
- accounts receivable
- research and development
- sales
- marketing
- technology and engineering
- production

In addition to the departments and functions above, you should also look at:

- suppliers
- distributors
- your physical location
- your physical assets, such as vehicles and equipment

Basic questions to ask in all of these areas include:

- What is happening in this area on a daily basis? (For example, is Accounts Receivable up-to-date on collecting for delinquent accounts?)

- Are the processes and procedures being used efficiently? (For example, are several employees unnecessarily duplicating work?)

- How could things be done better and more accurately? (For example, could the IT department help Research and Development document their findings more accurately?)

- Are costs being managed efficiently in this area? (For example, is paper being wasted because the copy machine needs to be repaired?)

- Is this area of the business flowing with areas it touches closely? (For example, is Customer Service aware of your AdWords and other advertising efforts before customers call in and ask about them?)

Competition and the Marketplace

Now that you have analyzed the status of your business, you need to analyze what is going on with your competition. This is important to every business and in any advertising plan, especially with AdWords, because you and your competitors will likely be bidding against the same keywords. You will be competing on many of the same search results pages. Easy price shopping and service comparisons are one of the benefits of shopping online, and you should be aware that your potential customers will probably be judging your ad, site, products, and services against those of your competitor before they make a decision to buy, or to even provide their contact information to you.

Remember, your competition is working to get the same customers that you are trying to get. They also are working to take the customers you have away from you to increase their revenue stream. Even competitors that you view as small or insignificant can affect your business. If your realistic goal is to increase customers in a geographic area by 100, and your small competitor gets 20 new customers in that same area, they have gained 20 customers that could have been yours. That is one-fifth, or 20 percent, of the gain that you needed to reach your goal. Despite the fact that AdWords has hundreds of thousands of users, it is a relatively new advertising medium and many of your competitors may not be using it yet. Use this to your advantage by starting your campaign, tweaking it, and growing before your competitors do. Get all of the business that you can through AdWords, and turn those customers, and the potential customer data you get from your AdWords campaigns, into targeted lists that your competitors have not even started to develop.

The following questions will help you organize information about your competition so you can make informed offensive and defensive decisions in your marketing strategy. Remember, your competition is any business or organization trying to get the same customers to buy the same product, use the same service, or donate to the same cause. If you do not know whom your competition is, conduct an Internet search for business categories that your business falls under. If you need some guidance for this, type in the name or label of your products and services or use the list from the Better Business Bureau® below. Doing a search for a category on this list may also give you some ideas for keywords or frequently used phrases that you can use in your own advertising.

The Better Business Bureau® organizes businesses into categories, which we will use to help determine your organization's focus and mission. Choose the category that your business falls into:

- arts & entertainment
- automotive
- business & professional services
- clothing & accessories
- community & government
- computers & electronics
- construction & contractors
- education
- food & dining
- health & medicine
- home & garden
- industry & agriculture
- legal & financial
- media & communications
- personal care & services
- real estate
- shopping
- sports & recreation
- travel & transportation

Through your research, you should be able to answer the following questions about your competitors:

1. Who is my current competition?

2. How successful are they?

3. What is the size of the market we are trying to reach?

4. Is the market flooded with competition?

5. Is there room to grow in this market?

6. Is the market stable?

7. Is the market constantly changing?

8. What percentage of the market share does the competition hold?

9. How are they marketing their goods or services?

10. What strategies are competitors using to market their goods or services?

11. How does their pricing compare to mine?

12. How does their product or service compare to mine?

13. What do I offer that they do not?

14. Why would customers choose me over them?

15. Why would customers choose them over me?

16. What is most valuable to my customers?

17. What amount are customers willing to pay for my products or services?

If the marketplace is competitive, which it probably is, it is important to study the performance of your competitors' marketing strategies. If they are publicly held companies, you can often find valuable information within online quarterly earnings reports, business publications, and special interest publications that serve your industry. Study what they do to market themselves. Learn from their mistakes, as well as their successes. Search the Internet. Look for information about the company and the marketplace. Get on their mailing list, if possible. Are they running AdWords ads? If so, what keywords are they using? Do they use these keywords over an extended period of time; say months, rather than days? That can show you which of their keywords may be successful or disappointing for them. *This will be discussed more in Chapter 8.*

Marketing

The ideal marketing strategy would be driven by an unlimited budget and would be fun to create and execute. And, with this unlimited budget, your consumers would respond to all aspects of the strategy exactly as you had planned, just as you would reach new consumers as planned. Real-life marketing strategies, however, are seldom driven by unlimited budgets. They are often fun to create and execute, but they are also a lot of work. Even with a generous budget and an effective message within a fun campaign, people do not always respond to your message. Marketing, advertising, and public relations should be a combination of art and science. Your marketing strategy, no matter your level of expertise in this field, or the size of your marketing budget, should reflect a combination of creativity and analysis. AdWords makes this simple.

For most advertising executives, the ideal marketing strategy would also keep your message in front of the right people at the right times consistently. In this case, after careful study of the message that should appear, you would employ every advertising medium, including direct mail, telemarketing, radio, broadcast and cable television, newspapers, magazines, blogs, content sites, Internet ads, billboards, e-mail, flyers, word-of-mouth, special events, promotional items, costumed characters, books, free gifts included in kids' meals at fast food restaurants, sponsorships of teams and events, celebrity endorsements, and neon signs in Times Square. If you have a budget that would allow you that option, then wow, you have a lot to do.

All of the advertising media above have their place within certain campaigns. They are all effective for different results and geared toward different targets at different places in the buying cycle. For example, billboards are most effective when used for brand recognition, for events, or to reinforce an idea being promoted elsewhere in the marketplace. Just because you see a billboard on your way to work every day, it does not mean that renting that billboard for your company's message is an effective marketing tool.

With AdWords, as with all of these other means of marketing, you can estimate and project results, but you really will not know how your advertising dollars translate into sales dollars until you try it. But, with AdWords, you can start with a $5 investment for your account setup fee and determine which keywords and ad offers get results. The initial financial investment in most of these other advertising venues is much greater than $5. The setup fees for many advertising options range in the thousands of dollars. For a small business owner with a limited budget, start small with an AdWords campaign, and, as your revenue builds, increase your AdWords advertising, and use these dollars to increase your advertising by also using these other venues.

There are a variety of ways to spend your advertising dollar. Most of them are effective, or they would not still be available. However, sometimes it is difficult to measure the effectiveness of different campaigns. Because of this, campaign tracking is important. Train your customer service personnel to ask new customers "How did you hear about us?" or "What made you aware of this special offer?" This can help tremendously. Promotion codes for discounted shipping or free samples entered at the point of sale (the place customers finalize their purchase) on your website, captures information about why an order is being placed, as well as motivates your customers to make the purchase. The way this works is every time a customer enters a promotion code, say XYZ, he or she gets a discount, free shipping, a free sample, or whatever the promotion code is offering. Then, when sales reports are run (most order-entry and bookkeeping software includes reports functions), you can see that eight out of ten sales with a promotion code used code XYZ. This code was included in a marketing e-mail you sent out, so you know that the offer associated with this code moved customers to place an order. You should definitely use that offer again.

With marketing, remember the little things often add up to your success. Changing one word in your AdWords ad can make a difference, as can using one keyword. To make a positive difference in your results, pay attention to the details of your marketing and advertising efforts.

Marketing strategy for your organization

Marketing strategy principles are the same for online marketing and traditional offline marketing. Creating ads and other creative components of advertising is just one step in an effective marketing strategy. Analyzing results and adapting your strategy based on those results is the best way to move a marketing strategy forward. In forming your marketing strategy, or to re-evaluate an existing strategy, ask the following questions:

1. How much money do I currently have budgeted for marketing?

2. How much am I spending now?

3. How much have I spent in the past?

4. What am I doing to market, or promote, my business or organization?

5. What have I done in the past?

6. Have I evaluated the results of previous marketing activities?

7. What were the results?

8. What was effective?

9. What was not effective?

10. What are my competitors doing to market their products and services?

11. Who are our customers?

12. Where do our customers come from?

13. What are our customers most interested in receiving from us?

14. What segments of the marketplace could be our customers, but currently are not?

15. How can we most effectively reach our customers?

16. Why would someone choose to do business with us?

17. Why would someone choose to do business with us rather than a competitor?

18. Is our pricing profitable?

19. Is our pricing comparable to that of our competition?

Please note that some of these questions are the same questions you asked regarding your competition. The answers to these questions are important in determining both where you stand when compared with your competition, and how you are going to effectively and positively differentiate yourself from them.

Based on the answers to these questions, you can develop a plan for your entire marketing strategy using Google AdWords as a cost-effective way to get results. *Use the worksheet at the end of this chapter to help you determine how to best use AdWords as a part of your overall strategy.*

What is My Budget for Getting New Customers?

Budgets can be determined by how much you have spent in the past, or simply by looking at what you have available to spend. Rather than thinking of your budget purely in a monetary sense, you should look at all of the resources in your business to determine what time, energy, personnel, and other resources, in addition to money, you have available to channel toward the marketing and advertising strategy you have developed.

AdWords account cost

There is a one-time fee of $5 to set up an AdWords account. There is no monthly or annual fee. Pricing options include cost-per-click (CPC) and cost-per-thousand impressions (CPM) pricing.

If you choose CPC pricing, it costs nothing for your ad to appear on a search results page or website. The CPC cost for AdWords is based on user response only. When a Google user responds to your ad by clicking on it, you are charged. This is the only determining factor of what your cost will be. If you have 2,500 impressions, 1,000 clicks, and only one sale, you pay for the 1,000 clicks. If you have 5,000 impressions, 1,000 clicks, and 800 sales, you still pay for the 1,000 clicks. The best way to decide between impressions or clicks is to determine the goal of your campaign. For example, if your goal is to remind people that your business can meet its needs, you should strongly consider impressions. If your goal is to drive people to your website to make a purchase, clicks will be a better option because you are paying for response with clicks, not for time in front of people, as you do with impressions.

If you use site targeting for your ad, rather than keyword targeting, you pay using CPM pricing. This means that your ad shows on your targeted sites X number of times. You pay for every 1,000 times your ad is shown on these sites.

Important key cost factors to keep in mind:

- The activation fee is a one-time $5 charge.

- There is no minimum-spending requirement.

- No contract is required.

- You determine how much you are willing to spend by setting a daily spending limit.

- You set how much you want to pay either per click, or per impression.

- You only pay when someone clicks on your ad that is keyword targeted.

- You only pay for impressions on your site-targeted ads.

- Your ad position is based on the maximum CPC and its quality score. *For more information on ad positioning and quality score see Chapter 8.*

Campaign budget

With AdWords, there is no minimum or maximum budget amount for a campaign. This allows businesses of any size to advertise within their own budget constraints by setting daily spending limits and by deciding how much you want to pay per click or per impression. Businesses in the same industry that offer similar products will have different budgets for marketing, advertising, and public relations efforts.

Determining a campaign budget involves a lot of variables. You may have several different campaigns with different budgets to promote different products or services that you offer. *For more about campaigns and this recommendation, see Chapter 6.* One of the important things to understand about AdWords is that you can continually change your monthly budget. This allows you to start slow and invest more money as you start to see results from your AdWords efforts.

Time, energy, and other resources

There is no guarantee that launching an AdWords campaign will propel your organization into a more profitable sphere of existence. But, when managed properly, AdWords can help you grow your customer base, generate leads, and help you expand your market in ways that many other advertising venues will not. Doing this will have some costs — which you control.

Besides the monetary resources, you need to invest to help your organization succeed in general and with AdWords, you should consider many other resources before launching any new advertising, marketing, or public relations effort. Time and energy are two of these resources. Time and energy translate to money. If you are spending time on tasks that are not productive for your organization, you are wasting time, your energy, and your money.

Financial expenditures, time, and energy should be considered in conjunction with other departments or functions of your organization. Before you launch your AdWords campaign, communicate with your entire organization. Communication is a challenge in organizations of every size. Let everyone know that you are launching a new type of advertising. E-mail the information, pass out handouts, and cover it in an employee meeting. Be certain that everyone from customer service to shipping knows what you are doing. They may have some valuable insight about preparation or keywords, and they may talk to customers who ask about your AdWords offer.

Worksheet: Developing an AdWords Strategy

Developing an AdWords strategy is quite similar to developing any communications or advertising strategy. Use the following questions to help you focus your AdWords message.

1. Who do I want to reach?

2. What do I want them to know?

3. What do I want them to do?

4. What about my product or service is valuable to them?

5. How do I reach them most effectively in AdWords?

Answers

1. Your target audience.

2. The message you want to communicate to your target audience.

3. This is the objective for your campaign.

4. This is the way to present your message to your target audience in a way that meets its needs.

5. This is the focus, or spectrum of your AdWords strategy. Please note that you may not fully know the answer to this question, but as you continue through this book, you will learn about the many options that AdWords makes available for you to reach your target audience with your message.

Chapter Four

Branding Your Organization for More Effective AdWords Results

Take a moment to picture some of your favorite things — your car, shoes, favorite jacket or shirt, your computer, your favorite handbag, cell phone, watch, and your favorite sports team. Now broaden your scope a little to consider some of the favorites of your family members, friends, or people you know — favorite gaming system, favorite television channel, favorite soap, cologne, cookware, detergent, even socks.

All of these items most likely have something in common aside from being the favorite of you or someone you know. They are probably a favorite because they are a certain brand. Of course, some people are more brand-conscious than others. In some cases, one brand may not be better made, more durable, or less expensive than a competitive brand, it may simply be the current, most popular brand. But, the quality of a brand can be an enormous part of its image and the perception that consumers have. Branding involves the perceived value of a product, service, company, or organization. In sports, someone's favorite team may not be the team that wins the most, but it is likely to offer a historical connection that involves emotions and memories — most likely a team affiliated with his or her hometown or alma mater. The value of the team is in the relationship, or the connection, rather than the win-loss record.

What is Branding?

Branding has a historical basis that comes from the practical need of determining the ownership of livestock. For centuries, livestock have been branded by burning an animal's flesh with a symbol that clearly noted who owned the animal and where the animal belonged. The brand on the animal would be recognized and tell the story of the animal. This type of branding is the precursor to the branding done in marketing and advertising today. Just like a livestock brand, your company's brand should be clearly defined and appear prominently in your promotions.

If you are not branding your company, products, or services, you are missing an opportunity to expand and solidify your audience. You do not need a huge marketing, advertising, promotions, or public relations budget to brand. You also do not need to be a professional in the promotions field to brand effectively. Being consistent in your communications, both offline and online, can give your audience a sense of who you are and, more important, who you are to them.

HOT TIP: Branding is all about image and the story that the image tells. It is a technique used to offer a consistent message to make target audiences respond in a desired way.

Your message to consumers is communicated by the way you brand, or represent, what you offer. Branding a product, service, or organization uses connections, including emotional, historical, visual, auditory, and psychological associations that should be repeated for consumers every time they see an ad, article, logo, product, or service associated with your organization. Understanding what makes a brand, and why it is important to use branding as part of your communications, is the first step to using this important strategy to increase awareness of your organization effectively, both online and off. Your AdWords strategy should include your branding focus to keep your message consistent, so it is important to understand how to develop your branding strategy and how to incorporate it into all of your communications.

Effective communication is based on trust. As a company, organization, or sole proprietorship interested in using Google's AdWords system for promoting your product, service, organization, or yourself, it is important to understand that consumers need to be able to depend upon the truthfulness and reliability of the message you are proclaiming. This basic idea is the cornerstone of all responsible marketing, advertising, public relations, and promotions of every kind.

If you are trying to reach distributors, suppliers, consumers, or volunteers, this message is the same: Trust what I offer, and what I say about it. These labels of "audiences" or "publics" you are trying to reach with your message are people. They are multi-faceted and are most likely interested in many things aside from whatever it is that you offer. Making a connection with an audience means making a connection with a group that is made up of people. Once that connection is established, delivering a message that continues to consider the person at the other end of the communication is essential. This is how trust is established, and this is how your branding message should be shaped.

This consistent message, using whatever type of media you choose, including AdWords, is the most important thing that can be communicated to your audience. This consistency is how customers become repeat customers

— they trust that their first positive experience will be repeated. You must repeat the experience for them if you want them to repeat their purchase, repeatedly visit your site, or repeatedly mention your product in their blog, or personally to other people.

Everyday branding

How and what consumers think about a company does make a difference. Brand loyalty is worth millions of dollars in revenue, especially to companies with stiff competition. The cola wars between Coca-Cola® and Pepsi™ are a prime example. These companies have launched new products, new packaging, and advertising campaigns to gain, or keep, the edge in beverage sales in the global marketplace. They have used advertising slogans and campaigns to try to identify closely with their target audiences and connect on an emotional level. It is interesting that they performed "taste test" campaigns many years ago, but have since focused on emotional appeal campaigns using slogans such as Coke's® "Open Happiness" 2009 campaign, and Pepsi's™ "Something for Everyone" campaign that began in 2008. These slogans do not focus on quality or taste, but rather on the emotional experience or feeling that the beverage offers. In this case, as with many branding opportunities, these two companies have focused on communicating the value of what they offer to consumers in a way that mass numbers of people can identify with and connect to. Their global market requires that they shift slogans and campaigns to consider language and cultural differences, but the message to consumers is the same: Your life will be better if you drink this.

Creating Your Brand

Rather than viewing branding as another item on your "to do" list, look at branding as an opportunity to communicate what you, as an organization or business, are all about. No matter what type of business or organization you are interested in making successful, a key component of that success is communicating how you are and who you are so your target audience can respond positively to you. Branding is a way to do this.

Branding is also a way to keep you focused on what is involved in your mission statement. By evolving your brand from your mission statement, and setting that as the framework for your branding, you allow your audience to connect automatically with your organization at its core.

Assembling and building a brand has a lot of similarities to assembling and building an intricate, multi-piece jigsaw puzzle. A lot of pieces must fit together to ensure that your message is consistent and that you end up with a smooth, cohesive image of what your organization means to the consumer. You start putting the puzzle together by first completing the outside edges. From there, you fill in the pieces that belong on the inside. If you look at your mission statement as the framework, or outside edges, that are necessary to hold the other pieces of your organization together, it makes the idea of branding easier to comprehend and implement.

The framework of your mission statement gives your branding an inherent credibility. The reason for having a mission statement is to clarify the purpose and reason for the existence of your organization. This reason should be reflected in the branding that you do.

The mission statement of Hotcakes Emporium is to offer products of superior quality and taste to its customers in convenient, easy-to-use forms. Note that the use of the word "products" allows for expansion beyond just hotcakes mix.

Branding equals consistency. Think of your name as your brand. When you introduce yourself to someone you have never met before, you tell him or her your name. The next time you meet with this person, you may need to remind them of who you are. You will tell them your name. Hopefully the next time you see this person, they will remember you and remember your name so that you do not have to re-introduce yourself. Your name identifies who you are. Your brand identifies your product or organization. It does not make sense to promote a product, service, or organization and continually reintroduce it to those who should already be able to identify it.

Your organization's personality

The personality of your organization should be a reflection of its mission statement and audience. What you are doing and whom you are doing it for make a difference. Your personality can appeal to some audiences and be a turn off for others. Most lawyers and others that offer legal services want their audience to see them as sturdy and reliable. That is why a lot of lawyers simply use their names as their logo, in a font with timeless, solid letters, to convey the personality of their firm. Even though the lawyers individually may have various personalities, the personality of their firm, because of the business they are in, needs to be one of trust and stability.

Another way to think of your organization's personality is "How does it engage people?" Think of this in terms of your personal relationships, people you know, and people you have observed. Personality plays a major part in the way others react to communication because personality often determines the way the communication is delivered. This is true in business, as well.

The personality of a children's museum should probably be different than that of a health care provider. But, if that health care provider is a pediatric dentist, there may be some similarities. In both of these cases, the organization provides its services to children. Children can be savvy consumers that influence buying decisions of a family, and appealing to this target market is an important consideration. Although it is the parents who typically provide the money for museum tickets and dental work, creating branding to appeal to both children and parents is important in both of these examples, because both children and parents are target audiences.

For Hotcakes Emporium, the overall personality of the organization should be fun. The goal is presenting the products as interesting, easy-to-use gift items, or for consumers to keep on hand in the event of a hotcakes emergency.

Developing a Logo

Once you have determined your organization's mission and personality, you are on your way to effective branding, a process that successful companies from FedEx to McDonald's to Nike have worked to develop over time. These recognized brands did not establish the association that consumers have with them overnight. Branding is a process. As with many introductions, the first impression is what people remember. This is where logos come in.

Each of the companies mentioned above have what is called "brand recognition," which means that they are easily recognized by much of the public. The logo that each has is integral to this recognition. The bold, block letters of FedEx, McDonald's golden arches, and the Nike swoosh are all images that are able to stand alone with no additional explanation.

The logo you use is just as important for your organization, no matter its size or scope. Note that having a logo is an assumption being made about your organization. It should not be seen as optional, because it is imperative to create a visual association that can be used both online and offline so your organization can be easily identified and set apart from your competitors. Please note that this information on logos includes the basics of what you need to create a logo yourself, or what to look for if you hire a professional.

> **HOT TIP:** "Logo design is a form of communication. The design must create an emotional connection to its viewer. Clean, simply designed logos will always stand the test of time." — Miles Parsons, creative director at Miles Parsons Graphic Design

Logos do not have to be complex visual artistic masterpieces. Sometimes less is more, and this is one of those times. By now you should know what you want your branding message to be. You understand how your message should reflect and communicate your organization's mission and personality. Do not forget that "please buy my stuff" is not the message that your audience wants to hear. Your audience wants to hear why they should spend money, time, or energy on what you have to offer. What are you offering to them? A logo is a great way to simply communicate what you do, what you offer, and your personality.

These questions, and their discussions below, will help you develop a logo to attract your target audience and tell the story of your organization. Questions you need to ask as part of the logo creation process include:

1. Do you want to use a symbol, the name of your organization, or both?

2. Do you want to use color?

3. Where will this logo potentially appear?

4. Will this logo be effective in five years? 15 years?

Question 1: Do you want to use a symbol, the name of your organization, or both?

You know what message you want your logo to convey. Now you need to decide what you want to include in the logo to convey this message most effectively. Do you want to use an image that suggests an aspect of what you do, what you sell, or what you offer to your target audience? Is there a simple image that can convey that message?

Keep in mind that if you choose to use an image, it does not have to be literal. Think abstractly. This image can, and probably should be, suggestive, rather than an exact image of what you do. A company involved in technology integration could have an image that includes several connected parts. This would be a more effective logo than if it cluttered the image with a tiny hard drive and wires in the logo. A waste management company would not be using common sense if they included a pile of trash in their logo. That is not attractive, is cluttered, and even though it represents what they do, the service they offer to consumers is a result of weekly trash pickup and recycling, which is to keep things clean. So, a simple logo with clean lines would be more appealing in this case.

Not using an image

An option with logo development is to use the name of the company without an image. This can be effective, especially when a font is used to convey an organization's personality. Juliet was romantic and poetic when she said in Shakespeare's *Romeo and Juliet*: "What's in a name? That which we call a rose by any other name would smell as sweet." She may have been insightful in love and romance, but with this thought process would not make it far in the current world of brand marketing.

The name associated with your products and services can be powerful. If it helps to convey your message to your target audience, use it to its fullest.

If it does not, consider amplifying its message by using imagery along with the name. The treatment of the letters in the name can make a tremendous difference in the way that your audience responds to you. The use of bold, whimsical, formal, casual, handwritten, traditional, or other types of fonts, can make a name feel like something your audience can relate to and automatically give the viewer a connection with it.

HOT TIP: Using fonts that include ornate letters can make more impact when you use only one letter such as:

 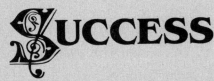

Using a line of picture letters can make a logo difficult to read and often does not translate well to small uses such as business cards. They may be cute or clever and convey your message, but if they are not easily read, they are not effective.

Question 2: Do you want to use color?

Color can make an impact. Cable networks include shows dedicated to the use of color in decorating, such as *ColorSplash*, which can change the mood and feel of people in a room. Other shows, such as *What Not to Wear,* focus on colors that should, and should not, be worn to determine fashion sense and flatter different body types. Color in a logo can also engage a target audience in different ways.

Find a color that supports your message. If your message is focused on generating excitement, red might be the color choice for you. If your goal is to calm and soothe, choose a shade of blue. Black, brown, gray, and white are considered neutral colors and can support your design in the form of a background, or can be used to make their own bold statement, especially in the case of black. Your organization might have a color that is naturally associated with it such as a vibrant green for a landscaping company or an ocean blue for a pool maintenance company. Another option for ensuring that your logo stands out from the competition is to use a color that is not typically associated with what you do. An example is a local waste management company that has painted its garbage pickup trucks a bright pink. Or, you could consider using a color that represents your personality if you are branding your own professional services. Either way, if you are using color, you may want to do some research to see how people respond to different colors.

HOT TIP: Make sure your logo is equally clear and impactful in black and white — create your initial design in grayscale, and then add the color.

Color can also be used to differentiate one product or service from another, or adapted within a logo for different promotions or specials, or both. Keep in mind that colors can mean different things to different cultures. If you are using color with your logo or other part of your AdWords or online campaign and may be reaching an international audience, do a little research before you make a color decision to ensure that a color that you choose conveys a consistent message to all cultures that your audience may include.

For example, the packaging for Hotcakes Emporium might include the logo in blue for its Blueberry Hotcakes mix, and in orange for its Harvest

Hotcakes. Many companies implement strict usage rules for their logo, regarding placement on a page, size, color, and black and white guidelines. This is done to ensure consistency with logo usage, and it reinforces the branding message.

Question 3: Where will this logo potentially appear?

Simplicity in a logo is crucial. Although you, no doubt, have many important messages to communicate, a logo is an opportunity to communicate visually and effectively the most important message that you have. Simplicity is important in a logo because it must be clear no matter where it appears, or what size it is. This is called scalability.

Consider how the logo will look blown-up or shrunk down to a tiny size in the following places:

- as part of an ad on Google's Content Network
- on product packaging
- on a billboard
- on a business card
- on the side of a delivery truck
- on your website
- on the back of a T-shirt
- on company letterhead
- on a coffee mug

HOT TIP: Do a test. Make a poster size version of your logo and mount it at eye level on a wall, on a tree in your yard, or prop it on your car. Take 30 steps away from it and then turn around. Can you read it? Is the image clear? Also, make it small enough to fit on a business card and check it for clarity and readability. If it passes these two tests, it should be easily scalable for whatever size you need it to be.

Question 4: Will this logo be effective in five years? 15 years?

Make your logo timeless. This does not necessarily mean traditional. But, unless you know that your logo represents a product or service that is going to be offered temporarily, keep in mind that making it too trendy, or too fashionable right now, may mean revisiting its effectiveness within a short time because fashions and trends change quickly.

Too much thought and work goes into a logo's creation to make it dispensable. With this in mind, you are not stuck with your logo for eternity. Logos can be changed. Businesses that survive adapt to their market. Logos can certainly adapt with them. But, effective branding requires consistency of message and a continually changing logo does not accomplish that.

Consider a visit to the grocery store to reinforce this idea. Products you buy repeatedly can be found easily on store shelves because of the packaging. Your favorite crackers may have a brightly colored box. Your favorite cereal most likely can be spotted initially because of the image on the front of the box. This grocery list of familiarity could go on and on to include cleaning supplies, coffee, pet food, dairy products, and most every type of product found on grocery store shelves. People repeatedly buy the same brands because they are familiar, because they have met their needs in the past, and are likely to meet their current needs. Being recognizable, with a timeless logo, has value whether that recognition takes place in a grocery store, on a billboard, or in an online ad.

Effective logo checklist

Use this checklist to help determine the effectiveness of your logo, so that you can make the right impression on your target audience through AdWords and in all of your promotions efforts. The answer to each of these questions should be yes.

- Is it simple?
- Does it communicate the essence of my organization?
- Is it scalable?
- Does it set my organization apart from its competition?
- Is the design clear in both color and black and white?
- Is it timeless?
- Does it allow me to expand my business?

You have seen the Hotcakes Emporium company (HE) throughout the book, walking you through examples of how a start-up company might use AdWords. Continue to use the HE example to move step-by-step through the logo creation process. This example can be applied to the creation of any logo.

After we established the mission and personality, we made a list of traits to convey what HE is all about. This fictional company is delivering a unique, quality, fun product. Consumer convenience is an important factor to the market. The reality check for this product is that it is a small bag of lightly colored, powdered mix. This could be boring and easily passed over by shoppers. So the logo — which will appear on the packaging, shipping boxes, and everything else — should be eye-catching, memorable, and make consumers want to know more. In this case, and in the case of many real everyday products, it really is all about the presentation. With these goals and considerations in mind, a logo design was deemed as a make-or-break factor in the presentation of this little company.

Should the logo include a symbol or only the name?

For HE, this was easy to decide. Luckily, the letter "O" is also the shape of a hotcake. Using this as a starting point, we examined several fonts, or letter styles. How much like a hotcake does the letter "O" actually look like? Some of the letters were too fanciful or were more oval-shaped, like an egg. Those were rejected. Some were too thin and were rejected because nobody wants a thin, runny hotcake. Thin fonts can be more serious or stark. The font finally chosen had an "O" that most closely resembled a hotcake shape and had a thick line, which reinforced not only the shape, but also lent an emotional connection of something familiar, easily related to and welcoming. Hotcakes are fun. Everyone is invited to enjoy them.

How should the font be handled?

With desktop publishing and printing options available, the possibilities of bold, underline, and italic are expanded to include an infinite variety of spacing, width, height, shadow, uppercase, lowercase, angled, filled in, shaded, and outlined decisions. Again, keep it simple. For HE, inviting and attainable were key concepts for this logo and the company's branding. Open fonts typically convey that mind-set while closed, filled-in fonts convey ideas more in tune with stability and sturdiness.

The font to use for the "emporium" part of the name was a little trickier. An emporium is a place to buy things, or, as Webster's puts it, "a store carrying a diversity of merchandise." The word emporium conjures images of a place packed with all sorts of interesting goodies and necessities. But, be a critic, and it can also produce images of old-fashioned places with lots of dust. Not what we want to convey. Without looking up this definition, consumers should understand that this is the place to buy something, and that they have options. To cancel out the possibility of the old, dusty image, clean and modern seemed the way to go. Also, the decision to keep it lowercase was made so it would not compete with the main focus — the hotcake.

So, now we have an inviting "hotcake" which is the focus, and a clean, balanced "emporium." Do they need to be side-by-side or stacked? Because hotcakes are typically served stacked, that is your answer.

Also, for the HE logo, because the majority of purchases will be made via online ordering, an instant appeal is essential. Because "hotcakes" is actually two yummy words smashed together, this also made lettering considerations a little easier. The selling point here is that lightly colored, powdery mix can be transformed into something delicious. So, now we have the reasoning behind the enlargement of HOT, which is now slightly more of the focus than the "cakes" portion of the word.

Can this be tweaked to become more effective?
Our HE logo now demonstrates the main criterion of logo creation. It conveys the message simply. But, it is not really memorable. To change this, we revisited our first priority: the hotcake image in the letter "O." This looks similar to a hotcake, but maximum hotcake enjoyment requires butter and

syrup. The butter is easy enough to convey in the form of a blob inside, or on, the "O." Squiggly lines to convey syrup meant that our simple, clean criteria for logos be thrown out the window. So, butter image is in, syrup image is out. But, squiggly, steamy lines work because they do not clutter the image, and they add depth both to the visual part of the logo and to the emotional connection: the smell and feel of warmth.

At this stage of the thought and tweaking process, which is when you think you have found your logo, the best thing to do is leave it alone and go to bed. Seriously, you need to sleep on it and come back to it when it has not been your focus for the past several hours. Doing this allows you to look at it from a fresh perspective and be critical of the impression it makes on you. The HE logo is close to completion now, but playing around with a box behind "emporium," reversing the letters to white with a black background, and letting the letters run into the white space behind the black background make it thoroughly done.

The best way to create a logo is to factor in your organization's priority, and then just play around with options until you get an image that conveys your message. Take a poll with friends, family, and anyone else willing to vote on which of your designs appeals to them the most. If you lack design sense, or do not have the time or patience to play around with logos and images, hire a professional to create a logo for you. Finding a professional designer with recommendations and a portfolio will be worth the investment. You can also hire one now that you are armed with plenty of information about logos.. This information also makes you savvy about the important responsibilities that a logo holds for your organization as you promote it through AdWords or any other medium.

Public perception

In the world of branding, perception is everything. The logo designed by your sister's child, who really wants to be an artist, may thrill you, but if your logo and branding message do not effectively communicate your organization's message to the audience you are trying to reach, it is pointless. Again, branding is an exchange between an organization and its publics.

One way to determine brand effectiveness is to measure your results. If your target audience is responding favorably to your brand by signing up, making a purchase, or requesting more information, you can make some positive perception assumptions. If response has leveled off or dropped, consider finding out why. The best way to do this is to ask.

The best timing for asking questions about brand effectiveness is before you launch your branding efforts. You can have an agency do marketing research for you. You can also do some testing with AdWords to determine the audience response based on a variety of options. You can also conduct informal, face-to-face interviews and ask members of your target audience to offer their opinion.

One of the benefits of AdWords is that you can change your branding message quickly and easily to generate the greatest appeal to your audience. If you are a start-up company, this is an inexpensive way to tailor your message to what your audience most wants and needs to hear from you and your products or services. Once you get an effective message out there, stick with it. If reliability is what consumers most want, be sure to integrate reliability into your message. If what they are looking for is quality, focus on quality.

It is important to get feedback from your audience once you establish a customer base, even if it is small. Ask customers what they like most. Ask them what changes could be made to improve your service or product. If you ask, you must listen.

You do not want your branding to be schizophrenic and change your message every time you receive negative feedback. But, you do want to consider feedback and determine if there are trends, or a comment or suggestion continually appears in your survey. An organization that adapts and thrives through the feedback of its audience has a greater chance of changing public perception into something positive that meets the needs of the business and the audience.

A word about licensing

An established brand is valuable. It has already been introduced and is recognizable. That usually means that marketing, advertising, and public relations dollars have been spent to move the brand from obscurity to a familiar place with its audience. So, other organizations that wish to be associated with, or partner with, an established brand pay for the licensing, or association. Sports teams typically partner with apparel manufacturers to include a school or team's logo on everything from hats and shirts to coffee mugs and pencils. The apparel and goods manufacturers are not owned by these schools, rather they pay a licensing fee for being allowed to include the school or team's logo on products that they make. The logo of these teams is a recognizable brand. This type of licensing partnership benefits the school because it receives a percentage of sales, and it benefits the manufacturer by increasing sales of its otherwise plain products. Licensing issues that involve infringement of licensing agreements or that disregard licensing requirements — use of a brand to promote something without permission — can be serious. Keep this in mind as you work to promote your own brand through AdWords and by other means, and get permission before you use another brand to help promote your own.

Chapter Five

AdWords as Part of Your Promotions Strategy

Even though you purchased this book to learn about AdWords, your branding and AdWords go hand in hand. The implementation of branding should not be limited to AdWords, but should be as comprehensive as budget and time allow. The reason is that branding efforts, whether offline or online, can serve as powerful complements of each other. Online branding options may initially appear to be easier to implement and easier on the budget, but the ultimate branding campaign would include every venue that will get your message in front of your audience. Because of that, your time and budget may be spent effectively on offline branding opportunities. Here are some things to keep in mind as you move forward in branding your organization.

Logo and contact information

Your logo should be on everything that you do both online and offline. If you are focusing primarily on operating an e-commerce website, you are probably sending information or products in response to those who access your online store. If that is the case, the logo that has been created to convey your message effectively, should appear prominently on any tangible and digital items that are sent to the consumer.

Keep in mind that your organization may be something that preoccupies your thoughts, and you feel passionate about it. It may be what you eat, sleep, and breathe. You know your website address and offer it instinctively to everyone you meet. Your target audience is probably not as focused on what you are doing as you are. Make it easy for them to find you again by including your message, logo, and contact information on whatever you produce, including your AdWords ads, landing page, e-mails, and other promotional and communications pieces.

Ordinary business communications

Printed materials provide an opportunity to include your branding message on an item that may be seen repeatedly by your audience. Some of these items are simple business exchanges that you may not consider as a branding tool. However, if you are producing a printed item individually from your ink-jet printer or in large quantities from a printing company, you have another opportunity to reinforce your message. If you can print on it, or in it, you can include it in your branding strategy. Examples of printed materials that you may produce that can, and should, include your branding message are:

- stationery
- business cards
- invoices
- packing slips
- receipts

Online advertising is a relatively new to the world of advertising. With technological advances, in addition to websites and other information being added daily to the already estimated 230 million-plus sites available, it appears that online advertising is here to stay. Businesses advertise and engage in public relations opportunities because there is a lot of competition for the attention and money of consumers. AdWords offers an easy-to-use, cost-effective means of getting the attention and money of Web users.

The number of Web users is estimated to be about 1.7 billion. This is a little more than 25 percent of the world's population. Of that 75 percent who are not Web users, many do not have access to computers. Those who have a computer and use it for Internet access may make up the majority of your target audience. But, until everyone on the planet uses the Web as a functional, integral part of their life, there are a lot of folks out there who may be interested in what you have to offer, but may not be looking on the Web to find it.

For example, an article in the local newspaper focusing on the amount of money collected in a school fund-raiser by selling Hotcakes Emporium products should include the website address. This article could drive traffic to the site and produce more orders. Likewise, a gift basket from Hotcakes Emporium is a featured giveaway in an online sweepstakes offered by a charity. Those signing up for the giveaway receive a confirmation e-mail including an HE promotion and link to the site, which increases interested traffic and, hopefully, sales.

One of the great things about taking advantage of a variety of branding opportunities, which include communications of every kind, is that they feed off of each other to create a positive snowball effect. Many of the opportunities considered as traditional, or offline, branding, marketing, advertising, and public relations venues have online counterparts. Many newspapers, magazines, and other print publications operate sites that offer advertisers the ability to advertise in both their print and online versions for discounted rates. Event sponsorships may include a logo on a T-shirt as well as a link to your organization on the event site. The chart at the end of this chapter offers a listing of branding opportunities and their offline and online availability. The following overview of other online branding opportunities should help you get an idea of what is available to complement your AdWords campaigns.

Other Online Branding Options

Although Google's advertising and branding options abound and reach a majority of Internet users worldwide, there are other online branding, advertising, and marketing opportunities to explore

Search engines besides Google

Yahoo!® accounts for about 14 percent of search traffic worldwide, while Bing™ accounts for roughly 10 percent of search traffic worldwide. This is a small number compared to Google's whopping 71 percent. The share covered by search engines other than Google is an estimated 200 million or more. Twenty-four percent of 200 million is 48 million search engine users, which offers an enormous market.

Microsoft® formed a partnership with Yahoo!® in early 2010 in an effort to tackle Google's enormous market share, but the outcome of this merger has yet to be seen. Yahoo!® modeled its "Sponsored Search" system after AdWords — much of it is the same. As of April 30, 2010, Yahoo!® no longer offers text ads for use and display on its search pages, but does offer display ad space on its network.

Bing™ and MSN® are also both owned by Microsoft® and link to each other on their home pages. If you select the advertising options for either search provider, you are taken to the Microsoft® adCenter®. Both also allow you to target demographics as well as search the millions of MSN® and Live Search users via Microsoft® adCenter®. They refer to target demographics as audience profiling. No matter the name, adCenter® allows you to determine the age, gender, geography, days of the week, and times of the day specifics for your target audience.

The main difference between these two search engines seems to be in layout and presentation. MSN's home page is loaded with boxes of information on news, sports, and other items trying to grab your attention. Bing's home page is clean and typically offers one image that covers the majority of the page. Bing™ treats Web information much like Google does, by dividing it into categories of travel, shopping, health, videos, history, news, images, and visual search.

An important difference between this and AdWords is that Microsoft® submits ads to an editorial review. The review is immediate and gives you feedback on your ad so you can adjust it while you are creating it. There are several reasons that an ad or keyword may not meet the editorial guidelines, including style: violating the phone number usage policy in your ad; inappropriate content, including hate speech, violence, online gambling, illegal activity, and adult content; products that are illegal, pharmaceutical, tobacco, weapons, deceptive products, and spam; trademark infringements; and working URLs and landing page.

After the online editorial review process, ads are submitted for approval and will not be posted until they are approved. You can change the ad to conform to the editorial guidelines or appeal disapproved ads and keywords. The benefit here is that grammar, punctuation, spelling, capitalization issues, and lack of relevance between your ad and your landing page can be corrected before your ad is posted.

Even though there are differences with each search engine, reaching your target audience with your message is your goal. You may reach more than enough through AdWords, but you may reach a more complete group of your target audience by branching out a little and by using what you learn through AdWords to positively affect your other promotions efforts.

An important note: The Ad Network available through Microsoft's search engines includes high traffic sites such as Facebook, while AdWords includes MySpace®, YouTube, and LinkedIn®. You can advertise on these networking sites individually or as part of the content network that includes them.

Individual sites

Although the content networks of the major search engines that you can advertise through may be comprehensive, they are not all encompassing. If there is a site that targets your audience that does not appear on your content network options, contact the site owners directly. The site owners may be interested in joining one or more content networks to expand revenue through ads on their site. Or, they may be interested in posting a link to your site for a fee. Keep in mind that your goal is to convert their site viewers into your customers, members, or information providers. Your purpose is to get people to your site to do what you want them to do. With this in mind, calculate your possible return on the investment of running an ad on an individual site. The site owners may be willing to charge you on a pay-per-click, cost-per-thousand-impressions basis, or offer you a flat fee. Calculate your ROI with the scenario they offer, and maintain the focus on your organization's goal before you commit.

Blogs

Blogs, which are "Web logs," or Web-based journals where the writer, or blogger, shares information that can range from specific topics (like the AdWords blog that can be found at **http://adwords.blogspot.com**) or can read more like the blogger's diary does. Either way, these blogs often accept advertisers' support in the form of payment for an actual blog post where the blogger writes about your organization or your product. It can also be in the form of an AdWords ad that appears on a blog as part of the Content Network.

You can also do your own blog to drive traffic to your site and to increase the possibility that your site will appear in a search. When planning your blog topics, use your keywords. This will increase the relevance of your topics and, again, increase the likelihood of bringing members of your target audience to your site. A blog should be considered a branding opportunity and can be used to inform existing customers, as well as to attract new customers.

Creating and maintaining your own blog is fairly simple using available software. Maintaining a blog and including interesting, pertinent entries is probably a blogger's greatest challenge. Like everything that you do, professional and business blogs should be created with the target audience in mind. Write on topics that will benefit your audience, and your blog is more likely to benefit you. Users may comment on most blogs and this is a way you can use your blog to help increase your leads. Requiring an e-mail address, username and password, to comment on the site will probably not bring in droves of new e-mail addresses to use as leads, but it may help.

Gaming

The video game, or gaming, community is continually growing. According to numbers appearing on the Microsoft® advertising site, advertising dollars spent on video game advertising in the U.S., which are targeting this predominantly male audience, are projected to reach $1 billion by 2012. Xbox Live and Xbox.com allow gamers that own these systems to purchase an Xbox game and play online with other gamers all over the world. Other gaming options found online, or played on computers, also offer advertising opportunities. Online game advertising, in-game ads, and social gaming events are advertising options you should consider if your audience is predominantly male, but you should also further research this option if your audience includes older and female members because they often engage in casual computer game play online.

Google terms the gaming community as an "emerging media" outlet, probably because it continues to grow. With AdWords, you can place your ads on gaming sites through the Content Network and earn revenue by allowing games to appear on your site via the AdSense program. *For more information on the Content Network and for more on AdSense see Chapter 6.*

Search Engine Optimization (SEO)

Search engine optimization, or SEO, is one of the biggest buzzwords in the online world. The World Wide Web is truly worldwide and the number of sites, blogs, and online postings of all types are seemingly infinite. SEO helps make your Web information a much larger, shinier needle in the haystack of online information.

SEO means just what the name implies — it optimizes your site's ability to be found by a search engine, such as Google, Yahoo!®, MSN®, Bing™, AltaVista™, Dogpile®, Lycos®, or other programs that search the Web for information. The real goal with SEO is to have your information, or site, listed on the first page of search results. Think about how you search. It is easier to click on a site that appears on that first page.

Although SEO and AdWords are separate components of your efforts to bring attention to your message, they can work together to create an online presence that expands your audience. The key to SEO, much like the key to AdWords, is keywords. The same keywords from your keyword research should be integrated seamlessly into the text of your site. This sounds pretty easy and is reminiscent of elementary school exercises where a vocabulary word must be used in a sentence. The reality is that keyword selection and content must offer real information. It also must flow coherently so that once a visitors comes to your site, they are not confused within five seconds because of the frustrating pseudo-information your site provides.

Do not be tempted to include a list of keywords on your site. This will not serve your customer's interest and minimizes your credibility. SEO is a component of the branding of your organization and providing compelling, relevant content is not only Google's goal, but it should also be yours, so you can maximize your credibility and offer value to those who visit your site. This also opens up the opportunity for repeat visits to your site.

There are a lot of books on SEO, and an amazing amount of information is available about this concept and attention-getting practice. There are also a lot of sites competing for the same keywords you want to use. Do not let that prevent you from using relevant keywords. But, with SEO, like AdWords, sometimes the less obvious and lesser-used keywords will bring sufficient results to drive traffic to your site and help you maintain a profitable business. Use the terms that appear on your keyword list that have good, but not the top, responses if using the top responses gets you bumped to the back of the pack.

An example of this would be if there was 30 providers of gourmet hotcake mix promoting themselves online. The keyword phrase "gourmet hotcake mix" is probably being used by all of them. But, they might not be using "yummy hotcake mix" or "best hotcake mix."

Advertising and Marketing Venues

A huge number of advertising and marketing venues will allow you to spend your money to promote your message and further your branding efforts. Use your money wisely to get the maximum response or bang for the bucks that you are spending. To do this, investigate response rates and calculate the projected return on your investment. Different target audiences respond in different ways so always, with everything you do in your ads, focus on what your target is most likely to respond to. This will help you select your message and your advertising medium.

Advertising sales professionals who offer advertising space for your message should be able to provide projected response figures and help you determine the best placement for your ad, and in many cases, design an ad for you. Be sure your ads and marketing efforts are graphically clean and easy to read. Clutter-free graphics and clutter-free copy go hand in hand. Copy, or the words you use in your ads, is typically more effective and understandable when it is straight to the point. Remember to focus on what the reader will gain from this information, just as you would in an AdWords ad.

HOT TIP: Call now! Get one before this offer runs out! Sign up today! Order yours! Don't be the only one without this! Act now! Only one more day of this special offer! and Buy now! are examples of calls to action that prompt a person to do what you want them to do and to do it while they are thinking about it.

When designing the graphics of your ads, remember that your goal is to draw the reader's eye through words, which are sharing your message. Many of these media are direct response; some will offer a more delayed response. An effective component of all advertising and marketing is a call to action, which can help get a more immediate return on your advertising and marketing investment. Tell the reader what you want them to do. Also, be prepared for big results by having staff and products to accommodate the increased business.

Public Relations Opportunities

Public relations, when compared to advertising and marketing, can be defined for your purposes as the way the flow of information between an organization and its publics is managed. The fact that those being communicated with in public relations efforts are considered publics, rather than an audience, is telling. An audience in the theater responds by applause, boos and hisses, or silence. They receive the message and react to it. A public, in contrast, is a group that shares a common interest, or may be considered a community. They are engaged in the message and help shape it rather than simply responding as an audience does to the message that is presented. Public relations professionals work to integrate your organization or business into the community and to show it in its most positive light while engaging the community in becoming a part of the organization. Because the work of communications involves marketing, advertising, and public relations, there is quite a bit of grey area between the fields and their responsibilities. For our purpose, we will define public relations as the flow of communications to portray an organization in its best light.

With this definition in mind, use a variety of public relations opportunities to contribute to your branding efforts. Establish your organization's expertise, using articles, how-to's, support of charitable causes, and otherwise to integrate your organization into the community. This can be done both on and offline, as the following branding opportunity chart illustrates.

Branding Opportunity	Use it Offline	Use it Online
Basic Business Forms & Communications		
Logo	x	x
Contact information	x	x
Packing slips	x	x
Invoices	x	x
Receipts	x	x
Shipping labels	x	
Stationery	x	x
Envelopes	x	
Checks / payments to vendors	x	x
Business cards	x	x
Folders	x	
Advertising & Marketing Venues		
Newspapers	x	x
Magazines	x	x
Special interest publications	x	x
Blogs		x
Social networking sites		x
Newsletters	x	x
Press releases	x	x
Billboards	x	x
Business directories	x	x
Television	x	x
Radio	x	x
Direct mail	x	x
Premium items	x	
E-mail marketing		x
Catalogs	x	x
Signs	x	x
Brochures	x	x
Flyers	x	
Delivery vehicles	x	
Uniforms	x	
Public Relations Opportunities		
Invitations & announcements	x	x
Memos	x	x
Letters	x	x
Gift certificates	x	x
Event sponsorships	x	x
Proposals	x	x

Branding Opportunity	Use it Offline	Use it Online
Annual & quarterly reports	x	x
Employee communications	x	x
White papers	x	x
Interviews	x	x
Speeches	x	x
Articles in publications	x	x
How-to's	x	x

Here are few points to keep in mind as you determine the best complements to your AdWords campaigns.

Newspapers offer sections with specialized content that can help reach a target audience. Newspapers vary widely in geographic coverage areas and in circulation — the number of people that read the paper. Most papers, no matter the size, have online counterparts that can also offer advertising space. Newspaper advertising can be expensive, but can generate trackable responses based on coupon ads or special offers. Besides including ads within the editorial sections of the paper, most papers offer insert opportunities for pullout ads that appeal to consumers searching for coupons and sales. Wednesdays and Sundays are usually the highest circulation days for daily newspapers, and many small, local papers have loyal followings.

Magazines and special interest publications can help you reach a specific target audience. As with all advertising, the more targeted the advertising, the higher result, and, in many cases, the higher the initial cost. Like newspapers, these publications typically have online counterparts and may offer package rates to combine advertising through both venues. Print publications also tend to linger on coffee tables and in waiting rooms and may be referred to repeatedly for information. This gives additional audience impact to advertisers.

Social networking sites, such as Facebook and MySpace®, continue to grow in popularity and offer ads in the form of ads that are similar to AdWords ads, plus you can use links to your site and your own network to promote your organization. Social networking sites are included in the Google Content Network and can be targeted through your AdWords campaign. Most social networking users are pretty savvy about advertising on these sites, so be considerate when you promote to your network. Constant marketing messages can be inconsiderate and will probably be ignored. Plan your strategy and use your network thoughtfully.

Television ads can be expensive, but when ads are scheduled to appear during shows your target audience watches, they can reap big benefits. Your options with television ad placement include Google TV ads as well as network and cable advertising. Network ads may bring a higher audience, but, of course, this is at a higher price. Cable ad placement allows your ad to show to the audience of specific shows, which are typically designed for a specific target. For both of these media, find a sales representative who makes you comfortable and will work with you to create a schedule that fits your budget.

Radio ads can be inexpensive to produce because there are no visuals required. But, you can create visual associations with words and sound. An example would be birds singing in the background to create an outdoor association. Effectively written radio ads with professional talent as the voice of the ad can provide great results. Morning drive times are the most expensive slots because that is typically the time radio shows have the most listeners. Many well-known radio hosts will integrate ads into their radio show and do the promotion themselves, which gives credibility to your ad, and also raises its price.

Newsletters are usually distributed to special interest groups, such as employees, clubs, churches, associations, and schools. Your organization can provide both printed and e-mail versions of a newsletter, or you can sponsor one that is already established. Having a story about your organization included in a newsletter gives you credibility with its audience, and newsletter editors are usually looking for fresh, relevant content to include. The key to a newsletter story is usually in doing something noteworthy with and for the newsletter audience.

Press releases are a way to announce a newsworthy event in the press, which may include print, broadcast, and trade publications. Press releases should be no longer than one page and should include contact information to make follow up easy for the reporter or writer of the story. Before you write and send a press release, research the publication and its audience to ensure that your information closely matches the interests of readers or viewers.

Billboards and other outdoor advertisements must be read by the average viewer in less than 30 seconds. Keep the word count to 12 or less and your message is more likely to be read. Choose the geographic area of your outdoor advertising carefully. The number of cars driving by may be impressive, but stay focused on those numbers as they relate to your target audience, so that your results may also be impressive.

Business directories such as the Yellow Pages, business.com, Google's Local Business Center (which includes Google Maps), and many others, are available in both print and digital forms and can be an effective way to reach the segment of your target audience that is actively searching for your products or services. Listings in both print and online versions of some of these may be costly. Many of them are free. Becoming a member of the Better Business Bureau® or its online division BBB*Online*, and asking a customer to do a rating for you on a consumer service site, such as Angie's List®, **www.angieslist.com**, gives you credibility and lets consumers know that ethical and trustworthy business practices are your operating standard.

Direct mail may be thought of as junk mail that clutters mailboxes, but it can get results. List companies can provide targeted lists to the smallest of targets. Direct mail houses often offer one-stop shopping of list generation, printing, sorting, and mailing and can tailor direct mail programs to fit your budget. Response rates vary with campaigns and target audiences, but a 2 percent response is generally considered strong. As with all advertising opportunities, consider your ROI before launching an expensive campaign.

Premium items include anything that a logo or message can be printed on, including shirts, jackets, coffee mugs, pens, umbrellas, note pads, and gifts. They can help your branding effort by serving as a reminder of who you are. Prices of items vary, and there are enough options available to allow you to choose items that will be used repeatedly by your target audience. These can be used for giveaways and can promote a specific product, service, or event.

E-mail marketing has a low cost of delivery and can help keep your branding message in front of your target audience. As with direct mail delivered via the postal service, your intent should not be to fill up a mailbox, but rather to deliver information of value that may benefit your customers or further engage recipients into the activities, events, and products your organization provides. Information on how to more effectively use the products and services you have already provided to them increases your credibility and reiterates that they made the correct purchase decision when they chose you as a vendor. E-mails can also be easily forwarded. Keep this in mind and include special promotions for discounts to customers who recommend you to their friends and family.

Telemarketing seems to be the most disdainful of advertising and marketing options. This is probably because telemarketers seem to call just when everyone settles down to dinner after a long day or at the climax of a favorite television show. But, advertisers would not use telemarketing if it did not work. Even though many households screen their calls, telemarketing can be effective because many people continue to answer the phone and make purchases this way. Purchasing a call database or listing, training and hiring callers, and providing phones lines for all can be rather complicated. There are companies that offer telemarketing services for particular campaigns. You can also find freelance telemarketers online.

Catalogs can be used both on and offline as a reference for your goods and services. Printed versions can be expensive, especially when printed in full color. They also may be referred to repeatedly because they typically offer seasonal or timeless, evergreen products that hold consumer interest. Online versions may still be expensive to produce if you use professional photography and layout services, but they give consumers a familiar way to view your products, just in a digital format.

Signs and posters are basic advertising media that are often overlooked. The restriction with them is that they are usually used to promote something in a geographic area. This is the case with yard signs that might announce work being done on a home by a landscape or remodeling company. Companies providing alarm services frequently use them. Other uses include store signs, which can be offered to retail establishments that carry your product and can be considered collectible works of art when they are done in neon or are promoted in a limited-edition format.

Brochures are most often used to pass along promotional information. The racks at visitors' centers and rest stops come to mind. These brochures are usually presented in a tri-fold format. Brochures, such as those found in doctor's offices, can also be a source of information. Headlines are important as a brochure's focus to tell the reader immediately what is available if they read your brochure instead of another. Design the headline so it appears in the space above the rack for maximum exposure.

Flyers can be an inexpensive and easy way to communicate your message. For the cost of paper and the time it takes to distribute them, you can promote an event, introduce a new retail store, and inform about an important topic. Flyers can be any size but are most often made by copying 8 ½ x 11 pieces of copy paper. To add a little inexpensive pizzazz to a flyer, use color paper rather than printing in colored ink. Be sure to check municipal regulations before placing flyers on telephone poles or in other public locations. Also, check with store owners before placing flyers on vehicles in a parking lot because the parking lot is considered private property and many stores prohibit distribution of any kind of solicitation on their property.

Delivery vehicles and uniforms can both help to promote your brand by reinforcing your message. Delivery vehicles could be included in the outdoor advertising category because they can be seen by large numbers of people in a geographic area. Uniforms can be as simple as khaki pants and a neat, clean shirt with a logo on it or can be theme-oriented to match the message of the organization. If you have people who interact personally with your target audience, consider using uniforms to reinforce your message with your customer.

Your imagination and creativity may show you advertising and marketing venues that specifically fit your organization and its promotions. A great example of this is a school lunch menu sponsored every month by a skating rink that provides the paper and makes the copies for distribution to every child in the school. It stays on the refrigerator all month and includes coupons and special events, along with the daily menu offering. This is an inexpensive way to reach the target audience, and it provides a service to the school, which gives the rink credibility and positive positioning. Look at what your target audience is doing and is involved in, and tailor your message and your medium to reach them in unusual ways.

Exercise: Think it Through

Use this exercise to help you move through the thought process to determine your organization's personality. This will help you brand your organization and reach out through AdWords, and any other promotional venue you choose, in a way that shows your target audience who you are and who you can be to them.

Personality can be interchangeable with some other words that can broaden your view of what an organization's personality entails:

- character
- identity
- qualities
- traits
- behavior
- tendency
- individuality

As you determine your organization's personality, use each of these words in place of the word "personality" to identify how your organization needs to portray itself to its audience and answer the following questions.

1. What type of character does my organization need to accomplish its mission? What is the most important attribute or feature needed?

2. What type of identity does my organization need to make it the most attractive to its audience?

- fun
- creative
- trustworthy
- whimsical
- cutting edge
- traditional
- futuristic
- cozy

3. What are the three main qualities my organization needs to exhibit?

4. What are the three main behavioral characteristics that my organization exhibits?

5. Choose your top three, in order of importance to your organization:

- create
- demonstrate
- evaluate
- locate
- measure

- move
- protect
- provide
- reproduce
- solve

6. Now, of the three that you chose, pick the one behavior characteristic that your organization should demonstrate over all the others. This top choice could also be picked by asking, "If we only did one thing and nothing else, what would it be?" If you offer a product or service, do not think of this in terms of the specific product or service, but rather as "What does this product do?" or "What does this service do?" for the consumer. This way of thinking helps put you in the mind-set of the consumer to determine the personality of your organization based on your target audience. If you are the sole proprietor of an organization, and your branding message is one you can strongly identify with, that is great. But, if your organization's personality and branding message does not speak to the audience that is going to keep you in business, it is not effective.

7. How can my organization best express its individuality and set it apart from the competition?

SECTION 2

AdWords Basics

Understanding the ins and outs of AdWords and how it can work for your business or organization is the key to managing and maximizing its potential. In this section, how the components work, and, more importantly, work together is explained in an easy-to-understand format. Once you finish this section, you should be better equipped to begin the AdWords process and begin making it a successful component of your promotions efforts.

Chapter Six

How Does the Process Work?

Now that you have established the mission, goals, objectives, budget, and branding for your organization, and explored the many venues for communicating your message, you can more easily focus your AdWords efforts to help your organization succeed. Your AdWords efforts will involve a lot more than signing up and writing ads. Your ad can look different and appear in many places. You can create many different types of ads and use AdWords to the fullest if you look at AdWords as a marketing system rather than simply as a place to post online ads.

Creating an AdWords Marketing Program

AdWords offers a lot of options and more are being added all the time. Use them all. Start small with text ads, then graduate to displays ads. Include your business information in the Local Business Center of Google Maps as part of the AdWords Content Network. Use YouTube videos as part of your efforts, and have your ads appear on YouTube. Remember that the key to effective branding and to communicating your organization's message is consistency. Using all of the business solutions available through Google and the AdWords system can help your organization meet its goals and objectives.

To cover this information, which is extensive, we will again use the Hotcakes Emporium (HE) company as our example and will do a sample plan for this business that you can adapt to the needs of your own organization. But first, look at the following graphic to visualize how the AdWords systems works, so that you can better understand how it can work for you. The rest of this chapter is organized according to this graphic so that you can find the information you need to create the type of ad to best meet your campaign goals.

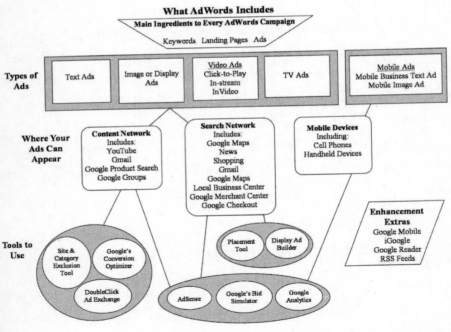

Keywords and landing pages are the main ingredients to the batter that makes up your AdWords campaigns. These two things would be the equivalent of the flour and sugar in the Hotcakes Emporium (HE) mix. Without these included and working in sync, your campaigns will not produce the results you are looking for, just as leaving out flour and sugar would prevent HE from having a wonderful hotcakes mix.

The other key ingredient included in each of your AdWords campaigns is the ad. Ads draw Google users to you and make it possible for them to connect with you. Just as baking soda in hotcakes mix makes the result light and fluffy, your ads give life to your campaigns.

Types of Ads

Adwords does not just offer the simple text ads, listed as Sponsored Links as Google users search the Internet for information or products. The AdWords system includes several types of ads that can be developed from within AdWords and displayed on its many network options.

Text ads

Text ads are simple four lines ads composed only of text. They do not include graphics of any kind, but proclaim, under a Sponsored Links heading, a headline, body text and a website address, or URL. Text ads are the basic type of ad used within AdWords and can be displayed within both the Search Network and the Content Network. *For more information on text ads, see Chapter 7.*

Google screenshots © Google Inc. Used with permission.

Display or image ads

Display ads, like text ads, can be continually optimized for best performance. A full website, called Google Display Network, is available to help you plan, create, and measure results of your display ads at **www.google. com/adwords/displaynetwork/**. The site includes information on setting effective bids and budgets for your display ads, customizing your ads, and trying different display options. According to Google, the Google Display Network consists of "all sites where you can buy ads through Google, including YouTube; Google properties such as Google Finance, Gmail, Google Maps, Blogger; plus more than one million Web; video gaming; and mobile display partners."

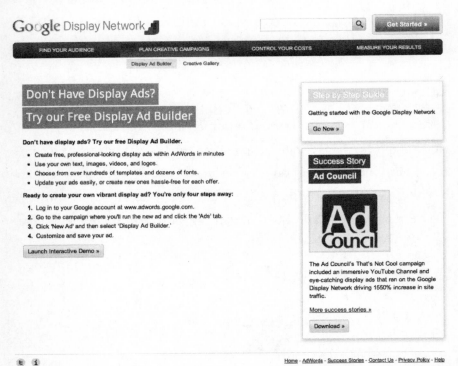

Google screenshots © Google Inc. Used with permission.

The first grouping of these terms are used for the overall AdWords system, and the following section offers a grouping of terms that apply to "placements," or where your ad may appear.

Video ad

Video ads can be used within the Content Network to engage consumers in a more interactive way. There are several types of video ads, which include:

- click-to-play video ads
- in-stream video ads
- InVideo ads

Your video ad can vary in length and, like other Google advertising options, you decide on your pricing model. You may choose between CPC and CPM.

TV ads

Google sometimes spends more than your per day budget. It explains this in the video that teaches more about how to set up a TV campaign. It also says it will not allow your spending to go over your daily budget multiplied by the days in a month. You need to determine your monthly budget for Google TV ads and divide that by 30. That way, you are not stuck with expenditures you have not budgeted for, especially in the case of a short campaign that does not last an entire month, or that ends in the middle of a month, rather than the end.

Mobile business text ad

If you opt to use mobile business text ads, also referred to as mobile ads, your ad may appear when someone using a mobile device does a Google search. These ads only appear on mobile devices and cannot be used on other Google sites, such as content or search sites. You cannot use local targeting with mobile ads, so your settings for these ads must target countries or territories. Because of this, it is better to create a separate campaign for this type of ad and to include keywords that make it clear where you are located, such as "Memphis plumbing."

Mobile ads are text-based, and contain only two lines of text with 12 to 18 characters per line. The third line of the mobile ad can contain your display URL, which will take users to your Web page. You can also opt to include a "call" link next to your display URL, which allows customers to connect to your business phone. The business phone number you include may not be a toll number and must be domestic to your ads' target location. As with all other ads submitted to AdWords, Google's editorial policies apply.

Once individuals click on your ad that appears with their search results, they go to a mobile Web page that you set up, or can connect directly to your business phone. You pay per click if they go to your Web page, and pay by call if they click on the call link. The cost to you, as an advertiser, for mobile ads is pay-per-click or per call. These ads are only available through keywords targeting.

You can also create mobile image ads. *See the Mobile Image Ads section for information about how to do this.*

Device platform targeting

Google has responded to the explosive use of mobile devices that use full (HTML) browsers, such as iPhones, BlackBerrys, and similar mobile devices by allowing AdWords advertisers to target these users with their ads. Device platform targeting (DPT) is a feature included in "Campaign Settings," which you can use to allow with targeting to desktop and laptop computers. Both of these platforms are targeted by default, but you can choose to disable this feature and target only computer users, or you can target only users of mobile devices that use full browsers. To activate a campaign, you must choose at least one of the device platform. Google's quality score criteria are applied to ads selecting either of the DPT options.

Please note that DPT and mobile ads are not the same. The difference is that with DPT, you are allowing your ad to be seen by users of mobile devices who use full (HTML) browsers; with mobile ads, your ads are formatted for display on mobile (WAP) browsers. Full browsers show your ad much as it appears if it were being viewed on a computer, while mobile ads must undergo specific formatting to be seen on mobile browsers. If you have opted to use mobile ads in your campaign, this campaign setting does not affect them.

Campaigns that use the CPT option of displaying on mobile devices with full browsers can show text ads on results pages of Google search and can show both text and image ads on the Content Network, if that is one of the campaign options you have selected. To get realistic data on how ads are doing on one device platform versus another, handle the ads targeted to each as separate campaigns. Your ads may be identical, but the platforms are not, so separate campaigns will allow you to track this, because Google's performance statistics will give you the results for the combined platforms.

This information is found by clicking the "campaigns" tab within your Google AdWords account.

Where Your Ads Can Appear

You must have at least one keyword for your ad to appear. This is because your ad appears in response to keywords in searches or on websites or any of the many options included with AdWords and its far-reaching Search and Content Network. *As discussed in Chapter 2, you can allow Google to determine where your ads appear, by using automatic placements, or you can manage and exclude your ad placements yourself.* The information below will help you understand what type of ads can appear in different places.

Content Network

The Google Content Network includes Google's search engine results pages plus websites, blogs, news pages, e-mail programs, YouTube, and any other Internet destination where the publisher has agreed to allow Google to include ads along with their content. According to Google, its Content Network reaches more than 75 percent of Internet users worldwide and includes websites numbering in the hundreds of thousands. Google's Content Network provides greater opportunity for the impressions that your ad receives to be relevant, and therefore, more productive for you. The Content Network greatly increases the opportunity for your ad to be seen by someone looking for information or wanting to buy your product. The Content Network also matches your ad's keywords and campaign data with the content that it matches most closely with that of its partners within the Content Network.

You can choose to advertise solely on Google's search engine results pages, or you can opt to have your ad also placed within Google's Content

Network. Because the Content Network reaches so many Internet users, Google has included simple customization tools to narrow down your ad's placements. Google divides these sites by industry:

- arts and humanities
- automotive
- business
- entertainment
- food and cooking
- health and fitness
- home and garden
- local
- men's interest
- music
- news
- online communities
- parenting and family
- politics
- sports
- technology
- teens/young adults
- travel
- women's interests

With the Content Network, your ad can be displayed on an astounding variety of sites, such as the Wall Street Journal, Reader's Digest, the Tennis Channel, Napster.com, NewsMax.com, foodnetwork.com, Smithsonian Magazine, Maxim Online, Neopets, and horoscope.com. Online communities such as MySpace®, LinkedIn®, Buzznet, Xanga, and YouTube are also available for ad placement as part of the Content Network.

The Content Network is a valuable way to target your Internet marketing on a wider spectrum. Having your ad show up on a national news site would be really cool. However, unless "show up on ten cool sites" is one of your measurable goals, stick with AdWords until you learn to manage campaigns through it. The Content Network also provides valuable analysis tools, but use AdWords first to determine which keywords and ads get the best results. Then, include those keywords and ads on the Content Network. With the information you gain from your AdWords campaigns, you can use the managed placement option more effectively. Managed placements allow you to choose specific sites from within the Content Network. If you do not have the time, or just do not want to pick these sites yourself, there is also an automatic placement option. The automatic placement option allows Google to target and match content with your ads.

HOT TIP: Google rotates text and image ads within the same ad group that targets the Content Network. The content of pages is also matched with the content of your ads and the closest match is chosen.

To get the most results from all of Google's Business Solutions, analysis is the key. *As recommended in the testing section in Chapter 11, keeping analysis focused on one component of your ad is crucial to make accurately informed decisions about ad effectiveness.* One way to prevent your ads that appear on the Content Network from blurring the information on your ads that are appearing on search results pages is to keep them separate. You can use the same ad for both. Keeping them separate, though, will allow you to realistically view the results on both and adjust your ads and their placement accordingly.

YouTube

YouTube is one of the world's most-viewed video sites, where anyone, anywhere with Web access and a camera can post videos, and, most important for AdWords users, ads. YouTube is part of Google's Content Network, so your AdWords ads can appear as a Sponsored Link next to a YouTube video. Hundreds of millions of videos are viewed daily, and new videos are being added daily so the keyword options with YouTube are endless. Video search results for YouTube operate through keyword search, just as Google's other search options. You can find videos by going to the "Videos" tab and searching a category.

Aside from offering display advertising alongside YouTube videos, InVideo ads are also available. These ads pop up as part of a video about 15 seconds into the video and appear at the bottom of the "watch screen" where videos are viewed. If a viewer is interested in the ad that pops up, a click will open up an ad video. Once the user finishes watching the ad, an icon is clicked and the video resumes where it left off when the ad was clicked.

Branding opportunities abound with YouTube and its branding channels. This is a place where your company can create engaging, brand-specific videos that can drive your brand recognition.

Gmail

Gmail, Google's e-mail service, is considered to be part of its Content Network, and, therefore, presents ads that might be displayed on any of its content partners online communications, such as Web pages or newsletters. The ads relate to both the topic of the e-mail and the content within the e-mail. (This is not quite as Big Brother as it may seem. Google's privacy policy allows only non-personal collections of information, such as how many users click on an ad through Gmail, rather than referencing the contents of your personal e-mail.)

Google Product Search

As online shopping options continue to grow, retailers large and small are turning to the Internet to offer products and services to consumers. Google Product Search is a part of Google's search engine that searches specifically for things to purchase. To access Product Search, Google users click on the Shopping link at the top of Google's home page. A search bar is available to type in products by name or type, and there is an area of the page that lists links with "a few of the items recently found with Google Product Search."

Google screenshots © Google Inc. Used with permission.

There is no cost to merchants for including products on Google Product Search, and it is a way to let shoppers go directly to the product that they are seeking. Products are uploaded through a data feed, and then appear on Google Product Search. When a shopper clicks on your product listing, they are taken to your site. If you have products that you can list on this shopping search engine, you may also want to include Google Commerce Search on your site. With this tool, shoppers can search your online store for products. So, check the shopping link to receive further information on how Product Search can help your business. Because it is part of Google's

Content Network, you can also use it to post your specific product and to have your ad appear within its search results.

Google Groups

Google Groups is Google's answer to social networking. The difference is that you can join types of groups, such as topic groups including (but not limited to):

- arts and entertainment groups
- business groups
- computer groups
- health groups
- home groups
- news groups
- people groups
- recreation groups
- school and university groups
- sci/tech groups
- society and humanity groups

There are also groups divided by region, messages per month, language, and days since last post. Google Groups is part of Google's Content Network, so you can choose which groups to target for your advertising message.

Site and Category Exclusion tool

The Site and Category Exclusion tool works within Google's Content Network. Websites where you do not want your ad to appear may be selected specifically by their URL and, therefore, prevent the AdWords system from including your ad within the site. Google automatically selects sites for your ad to appear on its Content Network. But, if you select the "site exclusion" option to go directly to the Site and Category Exclusion tool, go to **www.adwords.google.com/select/ContentExclusionStart**. You can also access this setting and choose which sites and categories you want to exclude from individual campaigns by going to the "campaign" menu from your account. Use the tabs to make exclusions, and then click "save all exclusions."

> **HOT TIP:** When AdWords implemented its 2009 interface, the exclusion tool stopped being fully supported. You can still exclude a category, but you can only view individual placement exclusions. So, even though it is working, you cannot see that it is working, so you may want to get around this by doing individual site exclusions.

Google's Conversion Optimizer

The Conversion Optimizer is a free tool for AdWords advertisers offered by Google to increase your conversions or results through your AdWords campaigns and decrease the amount it costs you to get a conversion or a result. According to Google's Help section, campaigns that adopt the Conversion Optimizer usually achieve a 21 percent increase in conversions while decreasing their CPA (cost per acquisition) by 14 percent. For advertisers, this means increasing results while decreasing costs.

This tool can also help you spend less time manually managing your AdWords campaigns. It does this by optimizing your campaigns for you as your campaign data changes and limits what you pay for your results. If you do not use this tool, you could get a thousand clicks that you would pay for and may get zero results. The tool allows you to place bids based on a maximum cost per acquisition, rather than a maximum CPC, or cost-per-click. So, you are paying for results, rather than attention to your ad by Google users. You still pay per click, but do not pay more than your maximum CPA for results. In order to be able to use Conversion Optimizer, you must be getting a minimum level of results from your existing AdWords campaigns. This assures Google that you are already making your keywords, ads, and landing pages relevant for users. You can access Google's Conversion Optimizer through your AdWords account or go to it directly at **www.google.com/adwords/conversionoptimizer**.

DoubleClick Ad Exchange

DoubleClick Ad Exchange is an advertising auction service offered by Google for large accounts and advertising agencies. On the "exchange," display advertising can be bought and sold impression-by-impression. The inventory on the "exchange" is part of Google's Content Network so it works seamlessly with your AdWords account. DoubleClick Ad Exchange expands your reach to more sites and, in practical terms, is an extension of the AdSense program. Participants in the "exchange" must adhere to AdSense policies, and publishers of sites allow you to include their site in your pool of potential "appearance sites" for an ad that you have created and posted on the Content Network.

Search Network

To understand how Google's advertising and business solutions programs work, it is important to understand how its searches work. The search engine drives the success of the advertising. The relevancy of the advertising to the search is what generates clicks to your ad and allows you to harvest information or turn clickers into customers.

You probably use Google, because millions of people use Google search multiple times every day. As discussed in the section on determining your target audience, you must think like the customer rather than the advertiser to tailor your message to your target. Based on that, focus on the Google users' experience to better understand how you, as an advertiser, reach your targets through Google.

When a user arrives at **www.google.com** to conduct a search, there are several options to select besides typing search words into the search box. Links on the upper left of the page include Web, images, videos, maps, news, shopping, Gmail, and more (with a tiny arrow beside it). You may click on these links to focus your search more specifically, or, if you leave "Web" as the default, Google's universal search gives you many of these categories within your search results.

Google screenshots © Google Inc. Used with permission.

As explained in the AdWords history section earlier in this book, Google clearly states and operates under the premise that its primary purpose as a company is to provide Internet searches. The amount of information available on the Web has revolutionized the way much of the world gathers information on topics that affect their personal and professional lives, such as products, services, people, and news. (For a chuckle, check out Google's 2002 April Fool's Day post on its patented PigeonRank™ system, which cleverly explains its search technology at **www.google.com/technology/ pigeonrank.html**.)

Rather than using the fictitious PigeonRank™, Google actually uses a ranking algorithm developed by its founders, Larry Page and Sergey Brin, called PageRank. PageRank, together with language models, query models, time models, and personalized models, forms the search system that consistently puts Google at the top of the search engine rankings. There is an enormous amount of information on the Google Help site, especially in the blogs. Google combines a variety of factors that work together to find search results within seconds. The complete formula is, understandably, top secret, but it all works together to maximize the relevancy of search results in response to millions of search queries.

As part of its quest to maintain its number one search engine status, Google launched Universal Search in 2007. Universal Search expanded search results to include grouped results of images, video, news, and maps in addition to the content pages that typically composed search results. Since its 2007 launch, Google has expanded Universal Search to include blog posts and book results. It also has added separate search products that include focused searches of blogs, books, finance, patents, products, scholarly papers, and many others, including the capability to search your own computer.

HOT TIP: Google offers a variety of special features to help you find what you are searching for. From an advertiser's point of view, the more exact the search results, the more precise your advertising is targeted.

CASE STUDY: ADWORDS HELPS CLIENT TAKE ACTION

ACTION ALAMEDA News
928 Taylor Avenue, Alameda, CA 94501
www.Action-Alameda-News.com
mowster@sbcglobal.net
(510) 673-0998
(510) 522-0231 fax
David Howard - Publisher, Webmaster

CLASSIFIED CASE STUDIES
directly from the experts

David Howard has used AdWords since 2002. He has managed several different campaigns over the years for small business, high-tech companies, grass-roots political organizations, a hyper-local news website, and political campaigns. He currently manages tens of thousands of dollars of monthly AdWords spending across multiple accounts. "When working on AdWords campaigns, I first identify the goals and objectives then flush out a budget and develop the campaign, including its ads [and] keywords lists. I offer the client guidance on landing page optimization then initiate and manage the campaign and check the numbers through reporting to determine the campaign's effectiveness," Howard said.

One of the accounts that he operated recently was for Action Alameda News and a local political campaign. The Action Alameda News site offers short-form news items from and about the city of Alameda, California. The budget totaled less than $500 per month. A portion of the budget, which equaled about 15 percent, was allocated to promoting campaign videos on YouTube.

The city of Alameda has about 75,000 residents. There was not a lot of competition on AdWords, but for this campaign, Howard had to compete against organic search, which included a lot of local bloggers with competing messages. Low competition made it easier for the Action Alameda ads to typically appear in the top position. The keyword list was continually developed throughout the campaign, drawing on data from Google analytics, potential key phrases from the mainstream press, and the competition's material. Bidding was focused on maximizing click through rate within the limited budget.

He reached his campaign objective, and Measure B, a controversial zoning initiative, was defeated at the polls. Overall, new visits to the site during the campaign were up 5 percent over the same time period in the previous year, which was a function of not only AdWords, but also news stories related to the campaign and organic search. There was a broad opposition campaign to Measure B mounted by a separate group that performed traditional campaigning, such as lawn signs [and] door-to-door canvassing. Howard's campaign was the only online effort in the race. Opponents to the measure were outspent on the order of 20 to 1, yet the measure was defeated by 6 to 1 in terms of votes.

"AdWords' analytical tools helped me with this campaign by helping me determine which ads provide higher click-through rates over time," said Howard. "They also helped me identify high-performing versus low-performing keywords and adjust bids accordingly, as well as determining ad positions and quality score to adjust landing page copy."

HOT TIPS from David Howard:

- The key is to identify objectives up front and a budget. How much are you willing to spend to achieve what results?

- Measure along the way to see if objectives are being reached, and adjust your campaign as you go.

- I highly recommend using the AdWords Editor desktop tool. It makes management, keywords, and bid changes a breeze.

- AdWords works hand-in-hand with organic search.

Search options

Google's primary business function is serving as a search engine. AdWords is a revenue-generating option used by Google to fund the maintenance of its search engine component. As the most widely used search engine in the world, Google offers a variety of search options for its users (**www.google.com/intl/en/help/features.html**), including:

- Everyday essentials: for finding the time for cities worldwide, weather, sports scores, and stock quotes.

- Reference tools: for accessing people profiles, Google's Book

Search, its built-in calculator function, public data trends for populations and unemployment rates, unit measurement conversions, and even recent earthquake data.

- Choosing keywords: for spell-checking software, finding dictionary definitions, and for finding synonyms along with your search terms.

- Local search: for finding business in a specific location, as well as showtimes for movies playing in your area.

- Trip planning: for accessing Google's built-in currency converter, for finding maps, and for airline travel info, including arriving and departing U.S. flights.

- Query refinements: for tips on how to pinpoint your search by having Google fill in the blank within your search, find Web pages that have similar or related content, and for including additional words that are essential to your search.

- Search by number: for finding the geographic location for U.S. telephone area codes; for tracking packages sent via FedEx, UPS, or USPS; and patent number searches for U.S. patents. For example, if you wanted to look up the band Lilyphone, you would have several options to choose from after pressing "search." To watch one of its videos, select the Video link on the Google home page; to search images of the band, select the Image link and continue the search process. When you search for it using the Web link, which is the search default, you see several search results written in Danish. You probably do not read Danish, but you want to know what this says about the band. So, from the Google home page, click on the "Language Tools" link to the right of the search box. When the "language tools" page comes up, type "Lilyphone" in the "search for" box. Select English in the "my language" box, and then select Danish for the "search pages written in" box. Then click on the "translate and search" button.

Web Images Videos Maps News Shopping Gmail more ▾

Google **Language Tools**

Translated search

Type a search phrase in your language. Google will find results in other languages and translate them for you to read.

Search for: Lilyphone   (Translate and Search)

Search pages written in: My language:
○ Automatically selected languages   English ▾
◉ Specific languages

☐ Afrikaans	☐ Estonian	☐ Italian	☐ Russian
☐ Albanian	☐ Filipino	☐ Japanese	☐ Serbian
☐ Arabic	☐ Finnish	☐ Korean	☐ Slovak
☐ Belarusian	☐ French	☐ Latvian	☐ Slovenian
☐ Bulgarian	☐ Galician	☐ Lithuanian	☐ Spanish
☐ Catalan	☐ German	☐ Macedonian	☐ Swahili
☐ Chinese (Simplified)	☐ Greek	☐ Malay	☐ Swedish
☐ Chinese (Traditional)	☐ Hebrew	☐ Maltese	☐ Thai
☐ Croatian	☐ Hindi	☐ Norwegian	☐ Turkish
☐ Czech	☐ Hungarian	☐ Persian	☐ Ukrainian
☑ Danish	☐ Icelandic	☐ Polish	☐ Vietnamese
☐ Dutch	☐ Indonesian	☐ Portuguese	☐ Welsh
☐ English	☐ Irish	☐ Romanian	☐ Yiddish

Example: 1. Search for Bern tourist information.
2. We translate your query into French and German, and find French and German results.
3. Finally, we translate the French and German results back into your language.

Google screenshots © Google Inc. Used with permission.

The Google translation page that comes up shows translated results from Danish Web pages. After selecting the "Release Lily Phone — KUBIK" document, Google takes a moment to translate, and you are able to read an article that covers the 2009 release of the band's debut album.

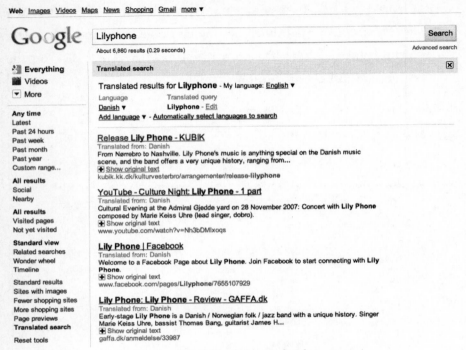

Google screenshots © Google Inc. Used with permission.

The Google translate search result pages currently do not contain AdWords ads, but the video search results page includes a listing with first frame images of the videos on the left of the page and features a much larger image with associated link to **www.youtube.com** to see the band's *Twinkling Of An Eye* video. Once the "watch this video on youtube.com" link is selected, you enter the world of YouTube, which is owned by Google, meaning it is included in Google's Content Network and is a destination for AdWords ads placement.

Understanding the search options that Google makes available to its users can help you, as an AdWords advertiser, more effectively reach your target audience. Understand how they search, and integrate this understanding into your keywords, ads, and campaigns to help them become more relevant to Google users. Additionally, you can use other components of

Google, such as Ad Extensions, AdSense, and Google Analytics to enhance your AdWords success. Remember, Google functions with a team of programs, not just one

Ad Extensions

Ad Extensions do exactly as the name implies — extend your ad. This is done by adding information to help those who see your ad find out more about your business, such as your address. Google recommends using ad extensions particularly when you have businesses in multiple locations, or when you'd like to attract more attention to your business when it appears on search results, including Google Maps, Google Mobile, and the Google Content Network. If a phone has an Internet browser or Google Maps for mobile, and your ad appears in a Google Map search, your ad can appear with the search results for the Google Map search because it has been extended to these media.

Ad Extensions are only added to standard text ads, which are shown using the AdWords ad criteria. An ad with Ad Extensions is simply a text AdWords ad with a little extra information included. You are charged for an Ad Extensions ad just like regular AdWords text ads, except when the ad shows on Google Maps. When the ad shows on Google Maps, you are not charged for clicks on your ad that expand the information windows on the map interface. Otherwise, if a user clicks to your website through your e xtensions information window, you are charged for the click-through. For more information about Ad Extensions, or to sign up, go to **http://adwords. google.com/support/aw/bin/answer.py?hl=en&answer=141826**.

AdSense

AdSense is the partner to Google's AdWords. AdSense is the service, provided by Google, that allows website publishers to display the AdWords ads on their site. AdSense is available in more than 12 languages. Google's system is a win-win for the advertiser and for the publisher of the sites. You can be both. As an advertiser, you can have one of your ads placed on your site, and if you have a site to promote your organization, you can allow other AdWords advertisers to have ads on your sites. When you are the placer of the ad, you are using AdWords. When you are the destination site for an ad, you are using AdSense. You can use AdWords and AdSense simultaneously to place your ads and to allow ads to be placed on your site.

Here is an example of how the cycle works: A Google user does a search. On the search results page, the user sees an ad for Hotcakes Emporium and clicks on the ad. Hotcakes Emporium is using the pay-per-click plan and will pay Google for this click. The user is dazzled by the array of hotcakes options on the Hotcakes Emporium page and orders a shipment of the frozen chocolate chip hotcakes for home delivery. After placing the order, the user clicks to the History of Hotcakes content page on the Hotcakes Emporium site. An ad for syrup catches his or her eye, causing the user to click on the syrup ad. Google pays Hotcakes Emporium for that click. The user has hotcakes and syrup on its way and has paid for both, meanwhile Hotcakes Emporium pays Google, and Google pays Hotcakes Emporium. In this example, Hotcakes Emporium is using both AdWords and AdSense and benefiting from both.

The more content on the Web, the more search results page options available. More content also means more pages and, therefore, more destinations for AdWords users' ads to appear. The incentive for a website publisher to enroll in AdSense is simple: Google does it all for you. As you change the content on your site, Google's search engine includes the content in its database to match the AdWords ad with the appropriate AdSense site. The AdWords advertiser pays Google when a site visitor clicks on the ad.

Google, in turn, pays the AdSense publisher when the site visitor clicks on an ad on its site.

Before placing an ad on a site, Google submits it to an ad review process to match the ad with the website's content as closely as possible, ensuring that the ad is suitable for all audiences and is a quality ad. If there are specific ads you do not want to appear on your page, such as competitors' ads, or those from websites you do not like, you can list those and Google will exclude them.

So that the ads appear as a seamless part of your website's pages, Google allows you to customize the colors of the ads that appear on your site. They offer a color selection tool that allows you to create your own custom palette from individual colors and preset color palettes, then save your customized palette to use with all of the ads appearing on your site.

Besides ads, you can also add a Google search box to your site, which allows your site's visitors to search your site and the Web from your site. *For more information about Search, see Chapter 10.*

You can track your AdSense earnings through your account. You can customize reporting options by ad type, ad category, URL, domain, and other groupings that you choose. As you track your earnings with these different options, you can determine which of these options are the most profitable. If there is a category that does not make you much money, you can try a different category. Like the information you get from the reporting features of AdWords, the AdSense reporting information allows you to look at what works to make money for you and what does not work. You can then optimize your AdSense options to develop a money-making addition to your site.

Google's Bid Simulator

Google's Bid Simulator lets you calculate potential impressions and clicks that you could receive with different maximum CPC (cost-per-click) bids. With this tool, you can get estimates on the traffic you can draw to your site through different bids. It is important to keep in mind that this tool offers estimates, not guaranteed results, but you can use it along with keywords in any of your AdWords campaigns to give you an idea of how a keyword might perform in conjunction with your CPC. You can access this tool through your AdWords account or access it directly by going to: **http:// adwords.google.com/support/aw/bin/topic.py?hl=en&topic=22217**.

Google Analytics

With Google Analytics, you can create custom reports and track conversions to give you the information you need to make your site as effective as possible. If your ads are generating a large number of clicks, but your conversion rate is low and the return on your investment is low, you should analyze your site to determine why users are not responding to the information it offers. The Google Analytics tool helps you do this by measuring your site's bounce rates and visits. *To learn more about Google Analytics, see Chapter 9.*

Google Merchant Center

This option allows its account holders to upload product feeds so they can be easily found on Google Product Search. For example, Hotcakes Emporium could use this service to allow Google users to purchase its gourmet hotcake mix, gift baskets, and any other product through Google Merchant Center.

This was formerly known as Google Base, which still exists for uploading non-product data feeds to help people find your items as they search via Google Product Search. You can use your uploaded product data in your AdWords ads. Your AdWords ads will also appear in Product Search results, so make yourself familiar with this option Google has provided for shoppers by going to **www.google.com/products**.

Google Checkout

Google Checkout is a one-stop shopping experience and destination for online purchases. This tool allows Google users to create one account and handle shopping, tracking, and shipping from a variety of stores through one site. The advantage it holds for AdWords advertisers is that it can allow you to attract more leads by being listed as a seller on this site. Google touts one of its benefits to sellers is an increased conversion rate, which it quotes as 40 percent more than with shoppers who have not used Checkout before. If you are selling a product, the Google Checkout store gadget allows you to create an online store to service the increased traffic that you should get to your site through using this service.

Fees for this service vary dependant on monthly sales volume. It ranges from 2.9 percent + $0.30 per transaction if sales are less than $3,000 to 1.9 percent + $0.30 if monthly sales are $100,000 or more. So, a quick calculation of these figures gives an estimated monthly cost range from approximately $180 to approximately $4,000.

Google checkout

Find it with Google. Buy it with Google Checkout.

Want a faster, safer, and more convenient way to shop online? You got it. Read about our buyer's experiences with Google Checkout.

Stop creating multiple accounts and passwords
With Google Checkout™ you can quickly and easily buy from stores across the web and track all your orders and shipping in one place.

Shop with confidence
Our fraud protection policy covers you against unauthorized purchases made through Google Checkout, and we don't share your purchase history or full credit card number with sellers.

Control commercial spam
You can keep your email address confidential, and easily turn off unwanted emails from stores where you use Google Checkout.

Search Google Checkout Stores

[_____] (Search)

Browse stores that accept Google Checkout.

Google screenshots © Google Inc. Used with permission.

Google Maps & Local Business Center

Google Maps offers directions and a focused way to find business addresses and places of interest. Google Maps is part of the AdWords advertising network, and your ad can appear alongside Google Map search results. So, Google Maps offers dual functionality to business owners in the form of advertising and as a business directory.

When a Google user uses the Search Maps option, search results, a map, and AdWords ads appear. Users can get car, public transit, and walking directions from this page and can choose if distances are shown in miles or kilometers. Users can search traffic, photos, videos, Wikipedia listings, area webcams, and real estate. The map can also be viewed via satellite and can include terrain. Users can use more than 1,000 options, including custom marker icons, GPS location, a distance measurement tool, favorite places, and Best of Citysearch®, to customize their Google Maps experience. New content options are offered frequently as Google continues to focus on provid ing the most relevant content to its users and advertisers.

Google Maps can display your business listing information at no cost, and you can advertise on Google Maps. Go to Google's Local Business Center **(www.Google.com/LocalBusinessCenter)** to update your business list-ing. When your listing comes up as a result of a Google Map search, a red pinpoint flag appears showing the location of your business. Red flags also pinpoint the location of other businesses that show up on the results page, which may include the location, address, and contact information for your competitors. Because your competitors' ad and listing probably appears in response to the same keywords and geographic search that you are in, you should customize your listing. You can customize your listing to include your business name, phone number, physical address, website

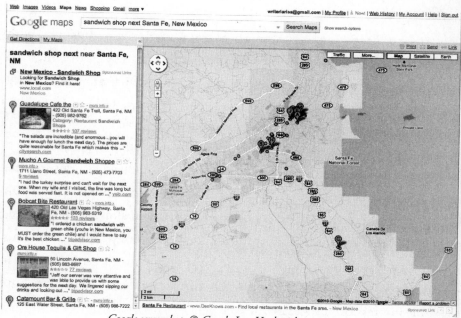

Google screenshots © Google Inc. Used with permission.

address, and e-mail address. You can add information that can set you apart from the other listings, such as parking availability, business hours, photos, videos, and acceptable types of payment. You can choose up to five business listing categories to explain your business. Google provides a list of category options, such as Asian grocery store, lamp shade supplier, wholesale jeweler, or gutter cleaning service, or you can customize your own.

Once your information is updated, you confirm your listing or make changes to it, and it is ready for posting. Google then gives you the option of receiving a phone call or postcard (which takes two to three weeks) to confirm your listing is correct.

> **HOT TIP:** Google Maps allows you to ad coupons to your Google Maps listing.

Local Business Ad

The Google Maps service offers a way to advertise your business with text-only ads that appear as users do geographic searches. An enhanced location marker shows with these AdWords ads, which are called Local Business Ads.

Ads are posted along with specific business listings on Google Maps. It is important to run "check changes" with local business ads to ensure that your ad matches the business location that you want. If you do not run "check changes" first, your ad is posted automatically along with the business listing that AdWords Editor most closely matches with your ad. This may be your business, and it may be your competitor's business. Or, it could take your customer across town and frustrate them rather than convert this impression into a sale for you.

FYI: If you attempt to post a local business ad that does not have a matching Google Maps listing, the ad will not be posted.

Quick Quiz: What Type of Ad Should You Use?

The concept of layering your organization's message by including it in many places that the same potential customer might see and get the message repeatedly is one that is common in advertising and marketing. The idea is that the more opportunities you have to reach your target audience, the better. With the many options involved in the AdWords process, such as the ones discussed in this chapter, you can easily manage similar, or unique, messages through several types of AdWords ads. Answer the questions below to measure your understanding of the process of selecting different types of AdWords ads.

1. How can you reach potential customers while they e-mail?

2. How can you reach potential customers on their mobile phone or smart phone?

3. How can you reach customers that are searching for directions?

4. How can you sell your products to potential customers who shop regularly through Google?

5. How can you potentially make money for your site by allowing other AdWords advertisers to advertise on your site?

Answers

1. Advertise with Gmail.

2. Use mobile business text ads and Device Platform Targeting.

3. Complete the information for Google Business Center and advertise through Google Maps.

4. Upload your products on Google Merchant Center and get traffic to your site through Google Checkout.

5. Participate in the AdSense program.

Chapter Seven

What Do I Do to Get Started?

Getting started with AdWords is relatively simple. This chapter will take you step-by-step through the sign-up process, including options and what you need to know to make the system work best for your organization. To do this, we will move through the tabs within your AdWords account and explain what to do, and how your decisions affect your AdWords promotions.

Google screenshots © Google Inc. Used with permission.

Home Tab

The "home" tab is, as with most websites, the place to get started. You can think of this tab as the home base for your AdWords activities. If you are new to AdWords, this is where you would begin learning about the process involved in budgeting, ad creation, keyword selection, and billing.

The first thing you need to do is register for your AdWords account. After initially setting up your login information, and subsequently every time you log in to AdWords, this is where you go. Once your information is entered, and you have started some campaigns, this tab includes an "account snapshot" page. It includes several categories of information, such as alerts, account status, announcements, a watch list, keyword performance report, campaign performance report, and helps and tips. This page is the default setting, but can be changed so that you go to the "campaign summary" page. To do this, select the box at the bottom of the "account snapshot" page.

HOT TIP: Allow AdWords to send you personalized ideas, special offers, and best practices information by clicking on the boxes that offer this. AdWords is continually changing and this information will help you stay current on how AdWords can help your business.

The "home" tab is also a place you can visit to help you get started on some advanced AdWords options, such as creating advanced campaigns, TV advertising, conversion tracking, and more. There is also access to links for commonly asked questions and a search option to search the help center for specific topics. To get help from any page within your AdWords account, there is a "help" link next to your account identification and "sign out" option at the top right of each page. So, you do not have to go back to the "home" tab to access the help topic you need.

For new advertisers, AdWords includes four steps to get started on this page. They are:

1. Choose your budget.

2. Create your ads.

3. Select keywords that match your ads to potential customers.

4. Enter your billing information.

Even though you do these things to get started, you must make many additional decisions about your ads before your ad is up and running. The preview available here will help you make these decisions prior to signing up, so your start-up process will go smoother.

Some of these decisions will be easier for some of you than others because of the nature of your business and campaign. We will cover your options and help you consider the benefits and drawbacks as we go. These options can be changed if they do not work for you, but it is easier to make informed decisions initially to avoid mistakes that could be costly.

Creating Your First Ad Campaign

When you click on the "create your first campaign" box, you will go to the "campaigns" tab. The first time you go to this tab, you will set up your campaign settings. After you set these up and then later return to this tab, it will appear differently because it will then be tracking your campaigns.

This tab allows you to create your first campaign. After it is created, you can use this tab to edit and organize your campaign into the following things:

- campaigns
- ad groups
- settings
- ads
- keywords
- networks

How it helps you:

- This tab is your go-to spot for reviewing your active campaigns.

- It allows you to create a new campaign and change the status of a campaign.

- You can create alerts to notify you automatically if you have an increase or decrease in specific metrics, or if, according to certain metrics, you have reached your predetermined threshold.

General

This is easy; just give your campaign a name. The name can be anything that helps you remember and easily reference its focus. Your first campaign will probably not be the only campaign that you run, so do not use the date for the name, but use one of these options:

- the product name you are promoting
- the name of the specific event you are promoting
- the name of the target audience for this campaign
- the special promotion you are offering
- the name of the service you are promoting
- the name of its purpose, such as lead generation, newsletter sign-up, or questionnaire completion
- the name of a geographic area

Using one of these options will help you with campaign maintenance as you add campaigns and include several ads under the umbrella campaign topic.

Locations, languages, and demographics

Choosing specific locations is a great way to start small and expand your audience, or to start big and narrow it down. For Hotcakes Emporium, we will select the "United States; Canada" location option because shipping is a consideration for customers who want to receive our product. We might expand this to all countries and territories later based on lower shipping costs to international locations.

To select specific international locations, click on the blue hyperlink: "select one or more other locations." This hyperlink takes you to myriad options where you can select a bundle of geographic locations within specific countries and regions. To give you a better idea of who may be exposed to your ad, a Google map that highlights the areas you have chosen appears on this "select a location" page. You can browse and search for specific areas, and also create custom options to show your ads within a specific mile radius to your address and can allow your address to show in your ads as well as exclude certain areas within selected locations. Under the "custom" tab, you can also use a feature that allows you to target a custom area for your ad's exposure by easily drawing your geographic specific geographic area or enter map coordinates. You can also paste or type up to 100 locations by selecting the "bulk" option at the top left of the page.

Once you are finished with your selections, make sure you save them by clicking on the "save" button in the lower left corner of this window. To return to the "campaigns" tab, click on the "X" in the upper right corner.

An "advanced" option included under the "locations selection" option allows you to show relevant addresses with your ads (advanced). You can use your address from your Local Business Center account or manually enter an address. *For more information on setting up your Local Business Center account, see Chapter 5.* If you include an address that is outside of your campaign's target area, it will not be shown in your ad.

Languages

Select the languages your customers speak here. You can easily edit the languages from the "default" option. With the "advanced demographic" option, if you are using the Content Network, this allows you to set bidding preferences, such as gender and age. Using these settings will generate traffic reports for the last seven days that you can use to further target your audience. *We will discuss this more in-depth when we review the "Reporting" tab in Chapter 10.*

Networks, devices, and extensions

This area is where you determine where your ad will appear. The devices option allows your ads to appear on mobile devices, such as phones and other handheld devices, such as BlackBerry® and iPhone®. Google defaults the networks and devices options in this section of the settings to "all available sites." The other option on each of these is "let me choose …"

Once you finalize the first campaign's settings, you can add more ads and ad groups within the same campaign or start a new campaign. To do this, go to the "campaigns" tab, and select the option you want ("new ad group," "new campaign," or "new ad").

Because of the increasing use of mobile devices, our fictitious Hotcakes Emporium business wants its ads to appear on them and sets up its campaigns accordingly. The idea behind this is that if HE can make its products available for users who want to buy a gift basket from their handheld device right when they think about it, then that option should available.

HOT TIP: Your campaign settings apply to each ad and ad group within the campaign. If you want to use a separate budget or separate location and language targeting, you must start a new campaign.

Once you have at least one campaign set up, when you go to the "campaigns" tab, you can view a list of all of your online campaigns. The "campaigns" tab is then divided into different tabs of its own which include: "campaigns," "ad groups," "settings," "ads," "keywords," and "networks." Each of these tabs allows you to look at a different aspect of your campaigns so you can see how all of these variables are working together to influence the success or failure of your campaigns.

For all of these sub-tab options that apply to your online campaigns, you can change your graph options to appear by clicks, impressions (shown as Impr.), CTR, average CPC, average CPM, cost, and average position. You can also choose to view these graph options by including one metric or two of them. This helps you compare useful information such as clicks and average CPC, impressions, average CPM, and cost versus average position of your ads. From each of these sub tabs, you can also view your change history, or check out changes that you have made in the past day, past five days, past month, past three months, past six months, and past year. Viewing your past changes may help you avoid costly mistakes and remind you why your CPC is different, when you added a new ad, a new ad group, started a new campaign, or ended one.

You can change the status of your ad groups under the "ad groups" sub tab to enable inactive ad groups, pause active ad groups, and delete ad groups. Something to consider before deleting an ad or an ad group is that the phrasing and keyword usage of an ad group may no longer apply to a specific product or service, but if you pause it, rather than delete it, you can use it for reference with other ads and ad groups. The ad groups that you want to delete may also serve as a helpful reminder of what did not work and why, so you do not duplicate your efforts in producing less than satisfactory results.

Also under the "campaigns" tab, the "settings" sub tab gives you options to set up the way your campaign information appears. You can include columns such as: campaign settings, location, language, networks, devices, bid type, end date, and ad scheduling. You can change the order of appearance for each of these columns by dragging and dropping its corresponding labeled bar. Once you save these settings, they will apply to all of your campaign information. You can also check the box next to a campaign name and change its settings or go directly to the information you want to change, such as budget, and click to change it.

An example of ways to make these settings work most effectively for you is to eliminate columns that apply to all of your campaigns. If the language for all of your campaigns is English, eliminating this column from your reports will not change the information you are receiving because it is all the same and does not need to appear in this information. Location and end date are other declutter setting options if your location is the same for all of your campaigns, and the end date you have set for your campaigns is none.

HOT TIP: The "ads" sub tab will show the ad that it is reporting for, which helps you compare all of your active ads at a glance.

You can edit your current ads as well as create new ads from the "ads" sub tab and also create a custom alert and manage your custom alerts. Custom alerts can help you track and manage changes in your ads or campaigns that you determine are important enough to you to receive a notification. Triggered alerts appear in your online campaigns information, and you can elect to receive notifications by e-mail so you will know that your campaign needs attention even if you are not working in AdWords. Alerts can be based on information such as the percentage of your daily budget that has been spent, cost, average CPC, CTR, average position, number of clicks, and number of impressions.

The "networks" sub tab under campaigns allows you to view your campaign results by Search Network and Content Network. The Search Network is subdivided into Google search and search partners, which can include other search engines that are part of Google's total Search Network. The Content Network results are subdivided by managed placements and automatic placements so you can determine how well the placement you manually selected on the Content Network is doing compared to the placements that Google automatically places for you. It also totals them both so that you can see how the networks compare and how they are working together.

> **HOT TIP:** To change active campaigns, go to the more actions button, which appears right above your keyword list. Select "spreadsheet edit" and from here you can add, edit, delete, or pause your keywords, edit or set keyword bids for individual keywords, and set unique destination URLs for different keywords.

The "spreadsheet edit" feature shows you the CPC for your ad to appear on the first page of search results. They vary widely, and this information gives you an opportunity to prioritize your keywords by how much you spend on each.

Your First Ad
(and if you are brave, your second and third)

Use the information in Chapter 8 for writing an effective ad. Then, immediately write another using the same keywords and settings. Google will rotate the ads you have in an ad group, and through this rotation, you can more easily determine what works and what does not. If Google users do not click on your first ads, rewrite them, wait for a week or so, and then take another look to see if anyone has clicked on your reworked ad. If you need to rewrite them again, keep in mind that your time and energy investment is making your ads more likely to bring the results you want and need. To help you keep your ads organized, they can be divided and categorized by ad groups.

Ad groups

Ad groups is the name of a tab within your AdWords account on the "all online campaigns" page. This tab provides an easy path to current information on your ads and campaigns, as well as a place to easily change existing ads and add new ones. Clicking on this tab will give you information on the groups of ads that you have in every campaign in your AdWords account. The graph on this tab shows the performance of all your ad groups and includes a "change graph options" link so you can customize the graph to see important data such as click, impressions, and average position. From this tab you can also sort information alphabetically, or from least to greatest, depending on the column heading. You can also go directly to ad group or campaign pages and make changes by clicking on the ad or campaign you want to change. You can make changes from here to the name of the ad group, to keywords, placements, and bids.

The statistics found on this tab include information you need to determine the effectiveness of your individual ad or campaign. Clicks, impressions, search, and content maximum bids are some of the statistics shown (all of these terms may be found in this chapter.) If you determine an ad is no longer effective, you can select the check box next to that ad group and delete or pause it. If you have paused an ad and would like it to begin running again, select "enable."

Setting Your Campaign Budget

You can edit your daily budget through the "campaigns" tab and set your budget according to your own criteria. A monthly budget may be the best option to use for this because most businesses and organizations calculate their financial statements on a monthly basis. Starting with a small budget is wise until you are able to tweak your keywords, ads, and landing pages, but you should keep in mind that you are looking for a positive return on your investment, and invest accordingly.

Effective bidding

Bidding is an important part of the AdWords process. *This is discussed more in depth in Chapter 8.* This component of the process allows you to stay within your budget and prioritize where your ad will appear. With bidding, you determine how much you will spend before you spend it. Determine your bidding strategy based on the goals of your campaign and if your goal is based on:

- the number of clicks your ads receive
- the number of impressions, or appearances your ad makes, or
- the number of conversions generated from your campaign

AdWords provides an automatic bidding option and other tools, including the Conversion Optimizer, Bid Simulator, and manual bidding to customize the amount of time and money that you want to spend on your campaigns.

The most commonly used bidding option is cost per click (CPC). Your bidding options include per click and per impressions. Bidding is done at the ad group level and the bid that you select for the ad group applies to every ad within that group by default. You can edit your bids at any time. The bid you enter as your maximum bid is the most you will pay. Google may match your keywords with searches that enable your ad to show for an amount less than your bid.

A cost-per-acquisition bid (CPA) is the amount you are willing to pay for results Google helps bring to your website. These results are typically a purchase or a sign-up. Conversions or results are the name of the success game, so this option may cost more initially, but you are only paying for results from Google users, rather than for interested Google users just looking at your site. CPA bidding is set up like the CPC bid process; you set a maximum amount that you will pay, and Google adjusts the amount you do pay by the costs it sets. This can sometimes be less than your max and sometimes, based on the number of conversions you have, Google adjusts your daily budget to include conversions that cost more than your maximum without exceeding your budget.

HOT TIP: Ask yourself what is the amount I am willing to pay for a new customer? The answer to this question will help you determine your max CPA bid.

Google encourages its advertisers to use automatic bidding settings. You can set an auto default bid, which is recommended for new AdWords advertisers because this maintains your cost at a level you can afford. Once you understand your target, effective keywords, and more about what initiates a response from your target audience, move to manual bidding. This gives you more control over placing a value on certain keywords and cuts down on the amount you pay Google for keywords that would be much less expensive.

Ad scheduling allows you to target certain hours and different days of the week for your ad to appear more frequently or fewer times. If you realize your ads are performing better at a particular time, you can increase your bid during this time. This allows you to pay more to be seen more. Rather than setting this bid increase at a specific max CPC, you include a bid multiplier for this time that can range from 10 percent to 1,000 percent of your normal bid. Setting the bid multiplier does not require you to change your max CPC for your entire ad group. It does allow you to increase your typical bid by a percentage during this time so you focus more money on this productive time and maintain your normal max CPC. This does not affect your budget, but it does affect all the ads in the campaign.

Hotcakes Emporium (HE) has realized that more orders are placed for gift baskets on Wednesday afternoons. So, it is important to have a gift baskets ad show during this time. The max CPC is set for the gift basket campaign at $1. Because orders are so prevalent during this time, it is worth paying $10 per click to ensure placement on the first page of the search results. Paying more than this amount will start to lower the ROI by too much.

HE inserts a bid multiplier of 1000 which makes bids go up to $10 because $1 x 1000% = $10. Now, on Wednesdays, with the bid multiplier, clicks may cost $10, but HE is able to increase its effectiveness by focusing on a peak ordering time, and the budget stays on track because Google adjusts spending within your budget parameters.

You do this by going to the "settings" tab and selecting the advanced settings section. Here is the step-by-step process to change your bid to include bid multipliers:

1. Click on "schedule: start date, end date, ad scheduling."

2. Click "edit" next to "ad scheduling."

3. Click "bid adjustment" above the table.

4. Click a row to adjust the bid multiplier for a period, click "OK," and "save" when you are finished.

To stop using the bid multipliers, go to the top of the ad scheduling window, and click "basic." Your multiplier settings will not be saved, but your time settings and max CPC will be saved.

HOT TIP: Connecting ads and landing pages is easy. When you insert your Destination URL into your ad text, it sets the location for a clicker's landing.

Providing your billing information

This process is fairly straightforward. You must provide your billing information before you can activate any ads in AdWords. An important note about Google's billing process: It accepts only its own numbers. If you are using a third-party reporting system and the numbers conflict with the numbers that Google provides, and, consequently, bills you for, Google's numbers are the numbers that will be used for your billing and any other reports. Google suggests that inconsistent times on the reports, or the fact that their software can detect clicks that other software cannot, may be the reasons for any discrepancy.

Quick Quiz:
Keep Tabs When Starting Your First Campaigns

1. Where do you go on Google to get started and begin learning about the process that is involved in budgeting, ad creation, keyword selection, and billing? (Hint: This may be thought of as your home base.)

2. Where do you go to begin your first campaign once you have created your AdWords account?

3. What are the three areas of your campaign you can adjust to broaden or narrow your target audience?

4. What is an efficient and easy way to monitor all of your campaigns? (Hint: You might do this to receive notifications on important campaigns.)

5. Where should you go to easily look at and manage all of your campaigns? (Hint: This tab will give you a group of ads for all the campaigns you have running on your account.)

6. How can you target certain hours or days for your campaign to appear on sites?

7. What is the information you must provide before you can activate your ads? (Hint: You need to pay for them before they will go up.)

Answers

1. "home" tab

2. "campaign" tab

3. location, demographics, language

4. custom alerts

5. ad groups

6. ad scheduling

7. your billing information

Chapter Eight

Getting Started with Google AdWords

If you are reading this book in order, and, no doubt, soaking in every word, you may be wondering how it is possible for you to be at the halfway point of the book and not have your first AdWords ad created, or even in progress. Be patient. If you are new to the advertising game, or new to the world of online promotions, all of this background information is forming a foundational understanding for you to avoid time-consuming, costly mistakes. With this information as your springboard, once you begin working in AdWords, you will understand much more clearly why you are taking each step as you move through the process. You will be prepared to make decisions based on the information you have researched and understand, rather than acting on a hunch and discovering a lot of this information through trial and error — or not discovering it at all and abandoning AdWords as an ineffective advertising method.

As you have learned, your basic AdWords tools include your keywords, ads, and landing pages:

1. Keywords initiate the relevant appearance of your ad.

2. The message of your ad compels Google users to click on it.

3. Your landing page prompts the user to act.

Research Relevant Keywords

Keywords are the foundation of everything you do in AdWords, and, for that matter, online, when you are working to promote anything from an idea to a product or service. Researching and finding effective keywords, are key to AdWords success. From Google's perspective, keywords help match search queries, or the needs of their users, with information and resources that respond to the search query and, therefore, meet the needs of their users.

From an advertiser's perspective, keywords help you find an online audience that is most likely to respond to the information you provide. This response could be in the form of a purchase, a download from your site, filling out a questionnaire, or providing an e-mail address to receive your weekly e-mail newsletter. Keywords can increase traffic to your site, and they can eliminate "browsers" who are curious, but not likely to take action on your behalf.

How you can research these words

Researching keywords is simple through AdWords. Initially, you should find as many keywords as you possibly can and then narrow them down. The first, and easiest, step in this process should be to use Google's Keyword tool.

CASE STUDY: KEYWORDS COME FIRST

Boost Labs, LLC
839 Quince Orchard Blvd., Suite M,
Gaithersburg, MD 20878
www.boostlabs.com
(301) 560-7901
(301) 560-1888 (fax)
Ali Allage — CEO

Boost Labs is a Web marketing and online brand-consulting firm that focuses on what separates customers' clients from their competitors. According to CEO Ali Allage, "We dive into their demographics to see what sort of keywords their potential clients are using. We also determine what keywords their competitors are using. We then determine their CPC and marketing budget to put together a campaign that yields a high ROI. The ad copy and landing page development comes next, and then we roll out the campaign."

Boost Labs runs two campaigns — one local and one national. Before starting any campaign, it calculates its max CPC based on its financials. In this example, the max CPC the company could afford was $2 per click. From there, it determined its yearly marketing budget and broke it down to a daily budget, which was $200 per day. Setting up the campaign, it plugged in the necessary financial info and went from there. With the CPC determined, the next step is to research specific keywords the company thinks it wants to use. Building a long keyword list is the focus before ad copy is touched.

Its initial keyword list is started from the keywords listing it got from Google Analytics, which are the keywords users are using via search. Then, the company starts searching to see if any of its competitors are using the same words. The initial keyword list then gets inserted into Google's Keyword program and more variations are pulled. The goal is to build an outrageously large keyword list to make sure any and all variations it may want to use are pulled.

The next step is to group the keywords into specific ad groups. As an example, Boost Labs has specific ads that run for its Social Media Marketing service, so all variations of Social Media Marketing keywords are placed into that ad group. Content placement in this example was placed to automatic because there was not a specific outlet to be focused on.

Once the ad group has run for a week, its performance is checked by determining the conversion ratio. If changes are made at this point, keywords that are not performing well are replaced, and landing pages are modified using multivariate testing to see if conversions can be boosted.

The company has been able to pull in 20 leads per month and able to convert one to two per month. So far it is seeing a profit from its campaign after all costs for both the campaign itself and the cost of doing the work. The ROI is 150 percent.

Hot Tips from Ali Allage:

- Put a lot of thought behind your landing page layouts and ad copy before starting a campaign.

- Budget is the most important element of developing an AdWords campaign. Not having the right CPC set puts you at risk for spending more on ads than you get in new business.

- Pay-Per-Click (PPC) advertising by far has been the most effective for us over other advertising methods. The only one that compares is actual face-to-face networking, but sometimes PPC outperforms that.

Worksheet: Keyword Brainstorm

Use this worksheet to help you find relevant keywords. (Make yourself a copy, so you can leave this worksheet blank in the book and use it to help you find keywords for multiple campaigns.)

In a true brainstorming session, there is no wrong answer. Some answers are better than others, but do not focus on why some of your keywords are better than others for this exercise. There will be time for analysis and prioritizing later. The point of this worksheet is to help you think like your audience, so you can reach it most effectively with your message.

For this exercise, focus on one product, service, event, sale, or promotion. Fill in the name of what you are focusing on in the line after "focus" below and in all the blanks in the worksheet. Answer the questions with this focus promotion in mind. Now take a deep breath, relax, and just write.

Focus: (include your focus here) _____

_____

Keep your answers limited to a maximum of five words each.

Features: What are the characteristics of (include your focus here) _____

_____.

1.

2.

3.

4.

5.

Benefits: How does each of the characteristics above help the target audience? What does each do for them?

1.

2.

3.

4.

5.

Features: What about (your focus) _____
_____ makes it different from what my competitor is offering?

1.

2.

3.

4.

5.

Benefits: What do the features listed above do to help the target audience? How does this feature help them?

1.

2.

3.

4.

5.

After completing this worksheet, you are learning to think like your target audience. Most people do not care if something is bigger or better unless bigger and better helps them directly. Google searchers are looking for help. That help may be in the form of information or a product or service. After completing this worksheet, you have a list of keywords and keyword phrases that you can test to determine what gets the best response.

Writing an Effective Text Ad

Text ads are the ads that appear as a result of a Google search. These ads are small and appear discreetly to the side, and sometimes at the top, of search results. They are labeled as "sponsored links" and give Google users an instant idea of whether you are offering what they want and where to go to get it.

Writing an effective text ad is key to AdWords success. The AdWords ad is where everything about your mission, your branding, and making money with AdWords comes into focus. This seems like a lot of pressure to be put onto 130 text characters that make up each text ad. But, these characters have helped the success of many organizations; yours does not have to be an exception.

If you have just broken out in a cold sweat because you have never written an ad of any kind before, mop off your brow, take a deep breath, and relax. With AdWords, you learn as you go. What makes an effective ad in one campaign may not apply to another. Changing ads to make them more effective is part of the fun and challenge of AdWords. The information here will help you leap ahead, and, although you may still have beginner status, you will be armed with tips and hints that have proven successful.

HOT TIP: Use your keywords in your ad to increase the chance that it will appear on the first page of search results, or in the top eight of ads that are shown, ultimately increasing the chances of your ad being seen by your target audience.

How to do this

AdWords text ads contain specific components and a limited number of characters in four lines of text.

Line No. 1 is the headline. It can include a maximum of 25 characters. It is used much the same way the headline in a newspaper is used to grab the reader's attention. Including one of your keywords in the headline is an effective attention-grabbing technique and helps to rank your ad higher in search results. Aside from being the attention grabber, the headline is also a link to your website or landing page.

Lines No. 2 and No. 3 are lines of text that have a maximum of 35 characters each. These two lines make up the meat of your ad. In these 70 characters, you have the opportunity to attract members of your target audience who are most interested in what you have to offer. If your goal were to generate as many clicks as possible, that would make this a little easier, but not nearly as effective. Remember that every click on your ad costs money. So, to get the maximum ROI from your AdWords ads, you want to eliminate those who are clicking because they are curious rather than because they intend to do what you want them to do once they arrive at your landing page.

Line No. 4 displays an address, or URL. This is the address of the site being promoted. For example, for a Hotcakes Emporium ad, this address would be **www.hotcakesemporium.com**. This line of text appears in green.

HOT TIP: The nuts and bolts of writing effective AdWords ads:

1. Make the headline an attention grabber.

2. Use the keyword for the ad in the headline.

3. Use the 70 characters on the next two lines to clearly explain what you are offering.

4. The text should attract consumers who want exactly what you are offering.

5. The text should also eliminate consumers who do not want what you have.

6. Your URL address should reinforce the message of your ad.

Newspaper headlines tell the story in just a few words and make the reader want to read more. Writing headlines for newspapers is an art form because space is limited, but the idea of a story may be huge. Readers make a decision in seconds about which stories they want to read based on the headline. The same is true for AdWords ads.

HOT TIP: Giveaways and the word "free" in your ad text will entice people to click on your ad. If that is your goal, you have found a way to reach it. If your goal, however, is to have them give you information, or make a purchase, you are attracting the wrong crowd. You are also paying for every time an uninterested browser clicks on your ad. Free can often mean lots of traffic, but very little return on your AdWords investment, so think it through before you include this common advertising word in your AdWords ad.

Using examples of other ads

Options for advertisers are seemingly endless. With advertising messages so prevalent, finding ads that help you create your own effective advertising is easy. Most advertising professionals are inspired by the creativity and perspective of their peers. An element of an ad on a billboard, in a newspaper, magazine, trade publication, on a television show, on the radio, on Google, or anywhere else you are exposed to ads can spark an idea that applies to your ad. Do not plagiarize or copy their ad, but borrow an element such as the headline, phrasing, call to action, graphics, and layout to customize and create your ad more effectively.

HOT TIP: When writing ad text, it is often helpful to ask these questions:

1. Are there identifiable trends in the ads that work?

2. Do particular calls to action, headlines, or description lines work better than others?

3. Can we apply successful ad text across the campaign?

4. Are users clicking on the ad with false expectations?

5. Should prices be reflected in the ad text?

6. Are users anticipating a sale or significant discount?

7. Are promotion specific ads timely and accurate?

For more information about writing ad text, see the Pacific Prime Insurance Brokers Ltd. Case Study in Chapter 12.

What if I cannot write?

Compelling, engaging, results-driven advertising copywriting can be great fun. With AdWords, mistakes can be caught early and easily repaired. But, there are many professional copywriters who can help you write text for your ads and your landing pages. These sites can provide information on professional help for your ad, campaign, and marketing strategy:

- **www.thewriteeditor.com** offers professional copywriting, editing, marketing, public relations, and management services and information.

- **www.g1440.com** provides online marketing, web design and development, web security, and IT staffing services, including search engine and conversion optimization.

- **www.hubspot.com** provides integrated online sales and marketing software and analysis.

Building an Ad

There was a time in history that building an ad meant placing a wooden block with a carved letter into ink and then stamping a piece of paper with it. This process was repeated with every letter, which made the process time consuming and tedious. The printing press changed all of that, and then the computer changed it all again. Building an ad to appear on Google's Content Network is very different from the beautiful, fine art of block printing, but it allows for some creativity and requires very little training.

Using Display Ad Builder

The tool that advertisers use to build ads to appear on the Content Network, which means they appear as part of a website rather than as a result of a Google search, is called the Display Ad Builder. The goal of a display ad is the same goal of a text ad: Draw someone to your site so that you can convert him or her to a customer or get information from them for a lead. The appearance is different than a text ad because both text and graphics are involved, which means you can use your logo, color, and different fonts to draw attention to your ad.

Once you decide to use a display ad and log in to your AdWords account, you can choose from different templates as the basis for your ad. A template is a predesigned model that you use to make your ad look similar in layout and design, and there are several to choose from. This means you do not have to be a professional graphic artist to create attractive, compelling display ads. Google has done several layouts for you, and they all include a headline, space for your logo, and a call to action. Most include an area for you to highlight a price and a product image.

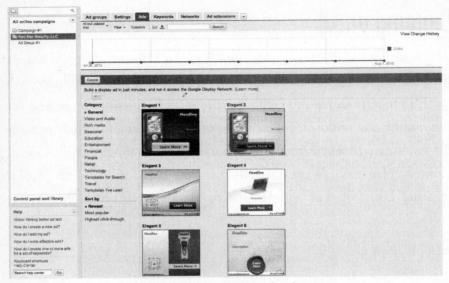

Google screenshots © Google Inc. Used with permission.

There are predesigned templates available with certain industries in mind. These templates include images that are related to a specific industry, such as financial services, technology, travel, and others. The logo and text, including headline and call to action, are customizable, but the images are preset. If you do not have an image you can download to your ad, this offers an attractive, viable display ad option for you. Even though the images in these ads may be industry specific, they may also apply to your product or the service that you are advertising. Check them out to determine if one of these templates, for an industry other than yours, meets your needs, and if it does, use it.

Many of the Display Ad Builder ads are built in a program called Flash®, which gives an ad movement through animation. For example, once an ad appears on the screen, the image may move into the ad from the left, or your logo may fade into the ad once the other components are showing on the screen.

The types of ads within Display Ad Builder are direct response and interactive. This means they both allow the user to click on the ad and go directly to your website or landing page. Other options include the capability to include a photo gallery as an integral part of your ad, a business locator that includes a Google Map of your location, a coupon layout, a site search option, an ad with integrated video, a product showcase, and several more things. According to Google, the idea behind the availability and variety of these ad templates is to engage the user in the information you are sharing. An engaging experience helps you more effectively compete with myriad marketing messages in front of your target audience. It helps make you relevant by showing your audience what you offer, rather than simply telling them. That is why these types of ads are called "display" ads — they display, or showcase your message.

Once you select the template that you think will best promote your message, click on the "create" button underneath the ad and the "create an ad" page will open. On this page, you can name your ad, customize the color, headline, headline color, include a description, change the description text color, upload your logo, and upload an image that will appear on the ad. As you change an item, you can select the "update preview" button under your ad template to see how it looks with the changes you have made. If you do not like a selection you have made, you can easily change it.

With all of its options, Display Ad Builder gives you quite a bit of flexibility. But, it is not flexible when it comes to image size, which includes a graphic or a logo. Check the current size standards that are listed on the "create an ad" page to make sure that your image can be used. You will need to use photo or image management software, such as Adobe® Photoshop® or Google's Picasa™, to resize the image before you download it. Both Photoshop® and Picasa™ can be downloaded from their websites so you do not have to wait for a CD to be delivered, but Picasa™ is free and Photoshop® is not.

As with text ads, you will need a display URL that appears as a website address on the ad, and a destination URL, which is invisible to the Google user, but will take clickers from your ad to your landing page. Remember that your display URL is the website address that you want to show up as part of your ad. You must include a display URL in every ad.

Once you customize your template to include your color, logo, and image preferences, Google uses these settings to automatically build several display ad sizes so your ad will appear different ways on different sites. If the different ad sizes do not look like you want them to appear on a website, you can make changes to them, or not use that size. To eliminate a specific size ad from your ad rotation, simply click on the box with the check mark that appears in front of the name of the ad you do not wish to use.

When you are satisfied with your ad layouts, click on the "save ad" button at the bottom of the page, and the display ad appears as part of your campaign. You must include your campaign settings for these ads, just as you would for your text ads.

HOT TIP: Display Ads 101, a feature available in Google AdWords Help Center, helps you better understand how to effectively set up your campaigns that include display ads. You can access it at **www.google.com/adwords/displayads101**.

The display ads that appear on Google's Content Network can also be uploaded. You can create ads yourself, or have an agency or other advertising professional create an ad for you. Google uses standard Web advertising sizes that have been determined by the Interactive Advertising Bureau (IAB).

Ad Options — Which is Best?

Text ads and display ads are both good. Use them both. They are good for different reasons, but they both get your message in front of a relevant target audience. If you are new to AdWords, and especially to advertising in general, start with text ads. This will allow you to test keywords, test different call to actions, test different offers, and test different content that draws Google users to your site. If you do not have a logo or an image that effectively and professionally communicates what your product or service can do for your target audience, use text ads until you have a chance to build your logo or have a professional design one for you. Your ads represent your organization and clean graphics represent an important opportunity for you to show what you offer in a positive, compelling light.

Display ads give you more options. Options make these ads customizable and engaging, but they can also be options that demonstrate a lack of design sense or a lack of professionalism if they are not done well. As with logo creation, test your images by taking a critical look at them before you use them. Have friends, family, coworkers, or employees look at images that you consider using before you use them. A different set of eyes looking at your images from a different perspective can be invaluable. Honest, constructive feedback can make a difference in how your ads appeal to your target audience, so use this inexpensive testing and review option before you run your ads.

The difference in these ads is not only in how they appear, but also in where they are shown and the information they provide. After you test several text ads for a month or so, use the descriptive text from your successful text ads in your display ads. Use headlines from effective text ads in your display ads. Remember that text ads are shown only as a result of a Google search. Display ads are shown as part of the content network. Google reviews display ads for relevance, but your standard should be higher.

Your display ad will change the look and feel of websites that include it; however, this may be discreet. Do some research not only on keywords that are included in websites, but also research the layout and feel of these sites. This does not have to be an exhaustive research project, but look at and consider colors that may blend or contrast nicely on some of these sites. Always, always, always consider your audience when creating ads of any kind. If you like an ad, but your target audience is not drawn to it, then it is not effective. Create your text and display ads with information that meets a need for your audience and place your ads, which include your keywords, on sites that attract your target. These sites may be a little more costly, but the ROI from them is likely to be greater.

Creating a Valuable Landing Page

Your landing page is where the "clicker" goes when they click on your ad. It is where they "land" to experience what you offered in your ad. The "destination URL" that you include when you create a text or display ad determines the landing page for each ad. Even though this destination URL is invisible to the clicker, it is an important part of your Google advertising effort because the landing page is the place where conversions happen. And, conversions are the name of the game. They are where you get the ROI from your ads in the form of sales, lead generation, or other information.

It is important to understand that Google places as much importance on the relevance and quality of your landing page as they do the relevance and quality of your ads. The criteria may seem rather stringent, but following the guidelines will help you create a landing page that serves your customers, and serves as a key component in an effective AdWords campaign. Landing pages are given a quality score by Google, just as they give quality scores to keywords — which affects each of your ads — and to content, both of which affect your positioning on both Google's search and content networks. The following is a summary of Google's minimum requirements for landing pages:

- Your landing page, otherwise known as your destination URL, must be in working order for you to use it with your ad.

- It may not be under construction, and it must work with any Web browser, and not be limited to use with, say, Firefox™ or Explorer®.

- Your destination URL must open without using an additional program or application. Examples of this would be audio, video, images, or document files that require another application to view or access.

Beyond Google's landing page criteria, you should have your own criteria for your landing page, focusing on conversions. Keep reading for more detailed information on effective landing pages.

What an effective landing page should include

An effective landing page should include whatever components you need in order to reach your measurable goals and objectives through AdWords. Every situation is unique for every business and every organization. Every AdWords ad and campaign is unique in some way. In every situation, the common aspect of every landing page is that it should be the place where you get the results from your ad.

Your landing page is your store. If you offer products for purchase, you want potential customers to land on the aisle that includes what they want to buy. If you offer services or information, give them the information they need. Do not expect them to wander through your online store or site, looking for the information desk when you promised information in your ad. Give them what you offer in your ad. The entire AdWords system is based on offering your target audience what they are looking for when they are looking for it. Keep this important point in mind when you design your landing pages.

Results-driven advertising is all about getting the results that your organization needs, such as closing the sale, signing up the volunteer, or getting the contract signed. When you persuade a potential customer to take action, a big part of your work is done. You have gotten their attention — big job — and you have written an ad that enticed them to move from the Web page they are on to yours — huge job. However, if the potential customer takes action and responds to your advertising efforts, and then you do not close the sale or get the results you are working for, you must take a good look at why the sale did not close. An offline example of this is when a radio ad generates calls to your call center, but the customer service representative does not close the sale. Some questions to ask when this happens include:

- Was it the price of the product or service?
- Was enough information given?
- Was this a case of information overload?
- Was the customer service rep not properly informed about the special offer?
- Was the customer service rep friendly?
- Did the customer service rep ask for the sale?

- Did the customer service rep make it easy for the customer to complete his or her purchase?

These are the same questions that you should ask about your landing page if a potential customer takes action in response to your AdWords ad, and then does not respond the way you need them to once they arrive at your landing page.

HOT TIP: Google Forms is an option you can use to collect e-mail responses and include them in a spreadsheet. You can also use this service, which is part of the many options in Google Docs, to retrieve information from your landing page or website.

Think of your landing page as the customer service representative who is commissioned with the job of getting the results from your AdWords campaign. Keep in mind that with PPC (pay-per-click) pricing, you are paying Google every time someone clicks on your AdWords ad. If you have a lot of clicks, your ad should be considered successful. If you have a lot of clicks and not a lot of sales, your landing page may be at fault — successful click rates do not necessarily equal successful ROI. *For information on how to know if this is happening, see the section on Conversion Rates in Chapter 4.*

The criteria that Google uses to determine the quality score of a landing page can be used to create an effective landing page. This criteria is listed below and explained in more detail following these bullet points:

- Be relevant.
- Be honest and transparent.
- Be original with the content on each landing page.
- Make it easy.

- Follow Google's advertising policies.

Be relevant. Relevance is Google's hallmark. Your landing page should smoothly transition from your ad. Answer the question posed in the clicker's mind when they click on your ad for more. Use keywords that are relevant to your ad to reiterate the fact that they have chosen the correct "sponsored link" or display ad to meet their needs. Take them directly to the page on your site that gives them what they want, rather than expect them to navigate your site in search of what they originally came for. Chances are, they will not do this, and you have just paid Google for a click that offers no return on your investment.

Be honest and transparent. An important part of branding is clearly communicating what you offer. Your landing page, as part of your branding effort, should provide the same standard of communication. For example, do not try to coerce your visitors to sign up for a newsletter, and then have them enter a credit card number to receive the free information.

HOT TIP: Google says it this way: "Be explicit in three primary areas: the nature of your business, how your site interacts with a visitor's computer, and how you intend to use a visitor's personal information, if you request it."

- *Be clear about the purpose of your business.* This does not have to take up an entire page or even include your mission statement. But, a short slogan or snippet that declares your purpose, such as "offering the highest quality, service, and ingredients," explains to the customer what you are all about. Ethics classes are taught in colleges and universities to share the ethics standards of businesses and individual professions. Using the highest standard of business ethics should not be an option, but, because that is not always the case,

Google specifically explains that you must honor the deals and offers in your ad, deliver products and services as promised, and only charge users for the products and services they order and successfully receive. Part of this transparency is also needed in ensuring that sponsored links and promotions are clearly identified as such and not integrated as part of your site's content without revealing that your organization has been paid for the inclusion of the information. Also, be clear about your pricing and billing information, and be obvious about billing and subscription information that involves recurring charges.

- Do not automatically install software from your site without the user's permission, and do not alter the user's browser behavior or settings without their permission. If your site installs software, provide clear, easy instructions for the software's removal.

- Do not request personal information unless you need it for the product or service you are offering. If you do request personal information, be clear, in the form of a privacy policy, about how it will be used, and give options to limit this information. A way to limit the information would be to allow them to opt-out of follow-up opportunities on your part, such as e-mail marketing or newsletters.

- Visitors to your site should be able to access its information without a registration requirement. If you do include such as requirement, give them a preview of what they will receive in return for their registration information.

HOT TIP: Google requires a mandatory opt-in box for recurring charges on the page where the user provides billing information.

Be original with the content on each landing page. AdWords will not show multiple ads that direct to identical or similar landing pages at the same time, so originality in a landing page is crucial for its availability with your ads. This applies primarily to distributors and resellers of products that may use similar sites to sell the same products. But, the rule of thumb here is that if an ad promotes something, its corresponding landing page should continue the user's experience seamlessly and meet the need of the user uniquely. If you are offering a product or service superior to that of your competitor, do not use a similar landing page. Take the time to customize and enhance the landing page to effectively demonstrate how you can be differentiated.

Make it easy. Users are coming to your site in response to something that enticed them in your ad. Make it easy for them to get what they came for. If you offer a product at a discount, include ordering information on the landing page. Also, avoid elements, such as pop-ups and pop-unders, that distract users from the business at hand, which is responding to your ad. It is perfectly acceptable to provide information on other products and services on your landing page, but do it in a way that keeps the user's experience positive and hassle-free.

Google also includes the time it takes for your landing page to load in its landing page quality score criteria. You can determine your landing page's load time grade in the keyword analysis field, which can be found in your account under the "keyword" tab. The status column next to any keyword offers this information. If your load time is too slow, and this affects your quality score, you can compress the size of your page, use fewer and faster redirects, and forego the use of interstitial pages. For more information load time improvement, enter "load time improvement" in the help center search within AdWords.

Follow Google's advertising policies. Google's list of advertising policies is extensive. A search within the AdWords Help Center for "advertising policies" will direct you to pages and pages of restrictions Google adheres to with its advertising. Do not worry about having to read and memorize these policies. The search result page within the Help Center includes a list of policies you can review and click on for more information if you think a policy will apply to your ad. When in doubt, check the list so you do not spend time and energy creating an ad, campaign, or landing page that will be rejected due to a violation of one of these advertising policies.

CASE STUDY: ADWORDS INVESTMENT GETS RETURN

Forever Films
17185 72nd Avenue North,
Maple Grove, MN 55311
www.ForeverFilmStudios.com
forever@foreverfilmstudios.com
(763) 898-3223
Charles Eide — Owner

Forever Films travels anywhere to capture weddings using cinematic videography. They travel nationally and internationally to shoot wedding films that are customized for each couple, so they can remember this special day for a lifetime. The company has managed several AdWords campaigns to promote its business.

Its Internet placement budget is $50 per day, which totals to about $1,500 per month with an average return of around $10,000 per month in gross revenue just from Google. It does this by selecting the few keywords that it wants and focuses on paying for them, rather than developing an extensive list. The number of keywords it uses ranges from about 25 to 50, and the company is very careful about using only targeted keywords. Also, it uses ads that are both specific and clear. The company's price range is included in each ad to prevent clients who are unwilling to pay for its service from clicking on the ad, because Forever Films understands that these clicks cost money without resulting in business. "We have learned that the more specific and clear your ad, the better your results," owner Charles Eide said. "Knowing who you want to attract before starting a campaign is something that we learned is really important."

Forever Films feels that knowing your audience well definitely benefits AdWords campaigns. "If you know how your audience thinks, what they like, and what they do not like, you can target them better. It works. Google has some great tools that help me find specific keywords that target my audience. I can even use Google tools to see what my competition is doing," Eide said.

A challenge that Forever Films faced as a small business was justifying its budget of $50 per day. But, according to Eide, "It only really works when you open up your wallet and have faith it will work. But, it does. It brought people to our site, and those who wanted us to contact them submitted a query on our site. Our goal was to get bookings and that is exactly what it brought. AdWords is more effective than other forms of advertising for us. It may cost more per exposure, but people who are interested go directly to our site."

HOT TIPS from Charles Eide:

- Use the keyword in the ad. For example, if someone searches wedding videography, our ad says "Forever Films wedding videography."

- Be specific and clear in your ads.

- Make sure your website is attractive. Having a good website is the most important part. Google's job is to get them to your site. It is your job to keep them there.

How a great landing page should be organized

Landing pages that include all of the components for effectiveness, but do not organize those components in an easy, compelling way, risk the loss of conversion. Some simple organizational guidelines can help you maximize the effectiveness of your landing pages, and, hopefully, the ROI of your AdWords campaigns.

A great landing page is key to successful conversions. Look at your conversion rate to determine the effectiveness of your landing page. If your ads are appearing and enticing visitors to your site, your landing page should deliver what they are looking for, and you should get conversions from it. If you have a low conversion rate, driving additional traffic is not likely to help you. Evaluate your website and landing pages if you are not converting the traffic that is coming your way.

A good product promoted by attractive, attention-getting, creative text and graphics that drives traffic to your site is exciting. Keeping that traffic at your site long enough for users to respond to your offer or request relies on the art and science of building effective landing pages.

Use simple layout and visual guidelines to help you organize your landing page.

- Use the keywords from your ad in the headline of your page.

- The headline, or focal point, of the page should include the reason the user clicked on your ad.

- Use visuals to draw the eye from left to right across the page.

- Keep the layout simple by not cluttering the page with too many graphics, images, or text that is difficult to read.

- Include your logo prominently, but do not let it be the focus of the page. The page's focus should be on delivering what the user needs or is looking for on your page.

- Use color. Keep in mind that the person looking at your landing page is also probably looking at lots of websites so yours should stand out. Using color helps to make your landing page more attractive and engaging.

HOT TIP: The Google sites tool can help you create a website, including landing pages, collect information from your site, and edit it. To access this tool go to **www.google.com/sites**. It includes pre-designed site templates, or you can develop your own from scratch.

Worksheet: Does the Customer Experience a Smooth Landing?

Generating a positive experience for the user, and a positive ROI for you is contingent on landing page effectiveness. Here are some practical ways to test your landing page:

1. Print out your text or display ad.
2. Print out your landing page.
3. Place them side-by-side.

Do they flow as if you were reading a book?

Does the headline or focus of your landing page directly address the reason a user clicked on your ad?

Can the user fulfill the purpose of visiting your landing page on the page or within the next two pages?

Is the text on the page easy to read?

Does the text on the page fit and further the purpose of the landing page?

Does the page include all of the components on the list below that you need for ordering, or for more information?

- customer name
- delivery address
- user e-mail address
- contact information in case e-mail address does not work.
- payment information
- an opt-in box giving you permission to send follow up information to the e-mail address, such as e-mail marketing or a newsletter

Chapter Nine

How do I Get the Best Online Presence through Google?

Google is continually adding products and services to help businesses succeed, which helps Google's business succeed. Being aware of all of these opportunities and taking advantage of them, while valuable, is time consuming. So, in response, Google has included an "opportunities" tab that is part of your AdWords account information. Once you set up your first AdWords campaign, Google analyzes it and matches it, and all your other campaigns, with opportunities you may want to take advantage of to increase your online presence, and your ROI. Taking advantage of the opportunities suggested is optional, and you should take a close look at them, and think about what they mean to your campaign and to your organization.

Opportunities Tab

The "opportunities" tab is a place where automatically generated ideas appear along with links to improvement tools found within AdWords. The ideas are automated, and the pages disclaimer advises users to review ideas carefully before implementing them. The goal with this section is to help you improve the success of your campaigns. Google is clear that its priority is to create a relevant experience for its users both through content and advertising, so the more relevant your ads and campaigns are for users, the better your response rate. This section also includes some general best practices information and campaign tips.

What you will find:

- a list of all of your online campaigns
- a list of ideas alongside their associated campaign
- access to AdWords tools
- access to help topics

Google screenshots © Google Inc. Used with permission.

The ideas generated here may apply to one of your campaigns, or to all of them. There is an option to show only your campaigns with ideas so you don't have to scroll through several of your campaigns to find one with an idea attached that will help you tweak and, hopefully, improve your campaign results. The ideas in the "opportunities" tab are examples of Google doing some of your analysis homework for you. It presents options along with an explanation of why the option is suggested. You can then immediately apply the idea to its associated campaign, or choose to ignore it.

Some of the tools you can access allow you to optimize your ads, analyze your ad performance, optimize your website, and manage your account offline. Some of the specific tools available from this tab include:

- keyword tool
- search-based keyword tool
- edit campaign negative keywords
- ads diagnostic tool
- ads preview tool
- placement tool
- Google's Conversion Optimizer
- conversion tracking
- Google's Bid Simulator
- site and category exclusion
- IP exclusion
- traffic estimator
- insights for search

Many of these tools can be used prior to developing or posting your campaign online. The "use before" tools include the keyword tool, search-based keyword tool, edit campaign negative keywords, placement tool, Google's Bid Simulator, site and category exclusion, IP exclusion, traffic estimator, and insights for search. If you use these tools as you are setting up your campaign, and before you put it online, you will have used your AdWords resources wisely because each of these help optimize your campaign before you start.

Remember, though, that the key to AdWords success is to continue analyzing, changing, and trying new ways to reach your target audience so these tools can also be invaluable to use after you have posted your campaign online. Using them while the campaign is running helps you analyze and change keywords, analyze and change websites where your ad appears, analyze and change the ads you are using, as well as change your bidding and campaigns goals.

Bidding strategies

The goal of a successful AdWords ad campaign should be to get the greatest ROI, or to get the most results for your business or organization for the least cost. Bidding is the key to managing the cost of your campaigns. You can use several tools and strategies to maximize the impact of your bids on your campaign results. These same tools and strategies can help you minimize the impact that your bidding has on your budget.

CASE STUDY:
TWO-FOLD ADWORDS FOCUS ON
SERVICE AWARENESS

The Healthcare Blue Book
330 Franklin Road, Suite 135A-428
Brentwood, TN 37027
www.healthcarebluebook.com
jrice@healthcarebluebook.com
(615) 377-6653
(615) 373-5295 fax
Jeffrey Rice, MD, JD – CEO

The *Healthcare Blue Book* is a free consumer guide to help consumers determine fair prices in your area for health care services. It allows health care patients find fair prices for surgery, hospital stays, doctor visits, medical tests, and much more by allowing them to compare prices and services between health care providers. The guide targets consumers who pay for their own health care, have a high deductible, or need services not fully covered by their insurance company. The guide targets consumers through AdWords in two different ways through two different AdWords campaigns.

The first is campaign is targeted to patients throughout the United States to help them find HCBB. This is considered the general awareness campaign. The HCBB site is offered for free to consumers, and it does not sell products. "We identify certain topics that we think are of most interest to patients and then develop keywords around those topics. The Google keyword suggestions can be very helpful and is an efficient way to capture a comprehensive list of keywords. We set budgets based on response rates and ad performance," said Jeffrey Rice, CEO of HCBB.

The second type of campaign the company runs is on behalf of HCBB clients, which include doctors, hospitals, and other health care providers who list their practices on HCBB to let patients know of their medical services. This second campaign is considered the client awareness campaign, and the company follows a similar method of keyword development. Monthly budgets for this type of campaign are fixed, so the company uses the budgeting tools in AdWords. "Actually keeping a campaign on budget requires continuous monitoring," said Rice. "We adjust the bidding amounts up or down periodically to keep the overall campaign on budget."

Narrowing down keywords for HCBB can be a daunting task, because in the medical field, there are thousands of services, which makes the number of potential keywords enormous. "We try to focus on the intersection of certain 'service' keywords, combined with our unique positioning around keywords related to value, which relates to HCBB's mission and positioning," said Rice. "We can determine level of consumer demand for certain topics and services that let us and our partners know where to focus attention on promotions.

AdWords helped a patient needing surgery find the HCBB service. She had been scheduled for surgery at a facility that was going to charge her at least $20,000, and after finding HCBB, she was able to keep her same surgeon and have the surgery performed in a different facility for a fixed rate of $7,000. We were able to help her save $13,000, and we paid only $0.17 for the ad that led her to our site," said Rice.

HOT TIPS from Jeffrey Rice:

- Keyword selection and managing a cost-effective bidding process are the most important elements in developing an AdWords campaign.

- Because you control the bidding and overall budget, you can feel safe about experimenting with the ads without incurring a lot of expense.

- To keep your campaigns on budget over a long period of time you can usually set your maximum CPC bid amount and total budget amount per day so the ad will run throughout the month at the rates you need to hit your monthly target.

AdWords Placement Terms to Understand and Implement

Where will my ad appear? That is one of the frequently asked questions of Google business solution users. The simple answer is that it will appear as a result of a Google search. The full answer to that question is that you decide where it will appear. Google bases ad appearance on the decisions you make on the type of placements you request, the type of ad, where you choose for it to appear in your settings, how relevant you make your ad, and how much you are willing to pay for good placement. Some placement terms that you need to understand are included in this section. This information will also help you understand why some of your ads appear in search results more than others and how to change that.

Ad rank

The ad rank is the determining factor in the positioning of ads in Google's search results pages and on their content pages. The higher the ad rank, the higher the position of the ad on the page. Your ad rank is important because when your ad is ranked on the first page of Google search results, it is more likely to be clicked by a potential customer or visitor to your site. That means potential revenue for you and potential revenue for Google.

Google uses a quality score system to rank its ads based on the relevancy of the keywords you select for your ad, plus other factors. That quality score combines with your maximum CPC to produce your ad rank.

Google does not allow advertisers to pay for top rank; rank has to be earned by the formula. This allows advertisers with any budget to obtain a top ad rank position. Since you cannot buy your ad rank, you must work to continually improve it. This system also ensures that your ads' quality is factored into its placement. This ensures that your ads actually get placed, even if they are not the highest bidder for a particular keyword.

Even though ad rank is used in both the search network and the content network, the criteria are different. For the search network, the ads are keyword-based so the ad rank is determined by this formula:

Ad Rank = CPC x Quality Score.

Several factors are taken into consideration for the quality score for keyword-based ads on the search network. They include:

- relevance of the keyword and the matched ad to the search query

- relevance of the keyword to the ads in its ad group

- the historical click-through rate, CTR, of the keyword and the matched ad that appears on Google

- the historical CTR of the display URLs in the ad group

- the account history, which is measured by the CTR of all the ads and keywords in your entire AdWords account

- your account's performance in the geographic region where your ad is shown, according to your campaign settings

- Google also uses other relevance factors. These factors are part of the information that Google holds as proprietary information that, if revealed, would give its competitors an edge in the search engine business.

Google will sometimes allow ads that exceed a certain CPC bid threshold and a certain quality score to appear above the search results. These ads are labeled "sponsored links" and are usually lightly highlighted to set them apart from the search results. Appearing in this area adds instant credibility to these ads because they are the first options that appear on the search results page. Google does not include ads above the search results in every search because the quality score and CPC bid threshold has not been met by an advertiser that is targeting the keywords or keyword phrase that generates the search results page.

The Content Network contains ads that are keyword-based and placement-targeted. The advertiser determines these settings when the campaign is set up. Keyword-based ads on the Content Network are positioned based on the ad group's content bid and quality score which translates in to this formula:

Ad Rank = content bid x Quality Score.

The quality score for the ad rank for ads appearing in the Content Network is based on:

- relevance of the ads and keywords to the site
- the ad's past performance on the site and other similar sites
- landing page quality
- Google also uses other relevance factors, which, like the unknown factors for quality score in search network ads, are held by Google as proprietary information.

For the placement-targeted ads on the Content Network, the formula used to determine if your ad will show on a partner site is:

Ad Rank = bid x Quality Score.

There are two different bid options for Content Network ads. They are cost-per-click (CPC) and cost-per-thousand impressions (CPM). For CPC bids on the Content Network, the quality of your landing page and the historical CTR of the ad on this and similar sites determine quality score. For CPM bids on the Content Network, quality score is determined only by the quality of your landing page.

To get your ads ranked as high as possible, do the following:

- **Bid as high as you can.** Whether you are using the Search Network or the Content Network, your bid is important in offering Google value for placing your ad in a top ranking position. Google will lower your cost based on your quality score, so if you bid high as your max, Google may eventually drop this rate, and a high ad rank may by worth the initial investment.

- **Make your ads relevant.** Bringing the most relevant information to its users is Google's main business goal, so it stands to reason that making your advertising relevant to Google's users will be rewarded. If you are choosing specific sites in your ad placement options, do a little homework, and make sure you include keywords from the site in your ad.

- **Create a great landing page.** Give the customer what they expect when they arrive at your landing page. If your ad is focused on a special offer for a product, allow the person that clicks on the ad the option to purchase the product on your landing page. If you offer something free, your landing page should immediately allow a customer to sign up for the freebie. Make it simple and easy, and both Google and your customers will reward you for it in the form of high ad ranking and increased conversion numbers. *For more information on landing pages, see Chapter 8.*

- **Maintain your account.** Because some of your rankings are dependent on the quality of your entire account, keep it clean and maximized. Pause or improve ads, groups, or campaigns that are not performing well. Doing this also helps your bottom line by focusing on results-driven ads.

Each of these things will increase your quality score, which will increase your ad rank. Most important, doing these things makes your customer's experience a good one and increases the likelihood that your conversions results will improve. Relevant, keyword-driven ads generate clicks. Good landing pages generate conversions. Conversions generate leads and purchases. This is the basis for business growth with anything you do in the Google Business Solutions System.

Google also has a tool called the AdWords Discounter that discounts the cost-per-click of your ads. This way you pay the lowest possible price for your ad's position, or rank, on the search engine results page.

CASE STUDY: HARVESTING MEMBERS THROUGH ADWORDS

BrainiacDating.com
P.O. Box 5145 Santa Clara, CA 95056
www.brainiacdating.com
lawrence@brainiacdating.com
Lawrence Chernin — Founder & CEO

BrainiacDating.com is a niche online dating site for smart singles. The site gained 15,000 registered members through AdWords in 15 months. To reach this goal, Lawrence Chernin, founder and CEO, created more than 100 campaigns and spent about $50,000. "Many of the campaigns were experimental. I experimented with different ad images, texts, keywords, and placements. The content network and its targeted placements were by far more cost effective for me than the search," he said.

Rather than continuing to fine-tune his campaigns, Chernin made each campaign and ad group unique so he would have clean and easy access to historical data. "Most of my success was with placements on one site, which more than 80 percent of my members came from. Unfortunately, the CPC then rose dramatically, and I was not able to continue to bid successfully on this site," Chernin said.

"The whole AdWords interface is very easy to use, and I like the fact that you can experiment with small amounts of money rather than committing hundreds of dollars to test something out, such as a new placement," Chernin said. He also found AdWords to be more cost effective than many print media sources that he tried. "The great aspect is that you can try out something on AdWords for $20 or less, while print media usually have minimum costs in the hundreds of dollars and up," he said.

A major challenge he found in AdWords is avoiding wasted clicks, because he did not want to pay for clicks for people that did not respond by signing up for BrainiacDating membership. "The ads need to show exactly what your product is, and I think this is also a key to the overall effectiveness of AdWords, because it encourages accuracy in advertising more than other media," Chernin said. "AdWords likes to have ads with higher click-through rates because they generate more revenue and will be given a higher quality score. So, you need to carefully target to get high click through rates and high conversion rates simultaneously."

Through this campaign, Chernin was able to gain some valuable insights into his target audience and was surprised to find much broader interest in his dating service niche than expected. "The fact is that there are a lot of people who would like to date someone smart even though they do not consider themselves smart. My website was never designed for this aspect, but it now accounts for almost 40 percent of the members," he said. "On the positive side, I learned that almost everyone wants to date someone smart, but on the problematic side, many highly intelligent people do not consider themselves to be 'brainiacs' — especially women." The information he learned about his target audience has helped him further target them through AdWords and bring more members aboard.

Hot Tips from Lawrence Chernin:

• The content network's automatic placements seeks out potential new placements that you wouldn't think of yourself by using your keywords and ad text to identify new potential sites.

- Be careful to put in the correct bid and not slip in an extra digit by accident. For example, I once bid at $10 instead of $1 and checked back an hour later and my $200 budget for the day was used up.

- The most important element of an AdWords campaign is the design of the ad image and text to avoid wasted clicks.

Quality score

Google uses a quality score system within AdWords to measure how effectively your ad is using keywords. A high quality score is the goal because Google discounts your CPC rate, and it means your keyword is triggering ads in a high position on the search results page. With quality score, Google gives you a discount for making your ad as relevant as it can possibly be. This benefits Google because a relevant match between an ad and a search results page, or a content page on the Content Network, is more likely to present the ad to a Google search user who would be interested in clicking on the ad. This produces revenue for Google when the advertiser pays for the click. It also gives the advertiser an increased opportunity to make some money as the search user becomes their site visitor.

You can improve your quality score by selecting the most relevant keywords for each ad within each of your campaigns. This is called optimizing your account.

Contextual targeting

AdWords uses contextual targeting within its Content Network to match the keywords that you select with content on an enormous number of websites worldwide. *For more information, see Content Network in Chapter 4.*

Quality Counts Worksheet

With AdWords, quality is important, and your quality score is an important factor in determining the placement of your ads. Placement and effectiveness are connected, so your quality score is important. Refer to the information in this chapter, and fill in the blanks below to help you remember what to do to maximize your quality score, and hopefully, maximize your AdWords results.

1. Bid as _____ as you can. (Hint: high or low?)

2. Make your ads _____ (Hint: what is an important concept in the Google search engine philosophy?)

3. Create a great _____. (Hint: where does your potential customer land after clicking on your ad?)

4. Maintain your _____. (Hint: the place where you log in to access your AdWords information)

Answers

1. high

2. relevant

3. landing page

4. account

SECTION 3

Analyzing AdWords

One of the things that makes AdWords easy to use is that it is easy to analyze its effectiveness. AdWords provides several tools for analyzing individual ads, campaigns, keywords, landing pages, and your bidding process. Understanding the payoff, or return on your investment with AdWords, can help you focus your efforts on specific target audiences, specific products and services, or special offers and text that draw higher response rates. At the end of this section, you should be familiar enough with the available AdWords tools to compare your AdWords efforts with your business goals.

Chapter Ten

How Do I Know it is Working?

This chapter will look at each of the analytical tools listed below, explain them, discuss how to read the results of each, and apply necessary changes to your campaign. Before we dive in to analyzing your results and measuring success, it is important for you to understand a few of basic concepts and analytical tools.

Ad position or rank

This term describes the position, or rank, of your ad as it appears in search results. The primary goal is to have your text ads appear on the first page of search results. High CPC bids and strong CTR, along with relevant ad text that responds to relevant keywords all work together to raise the position of your ad. Optimizing all of these factors in each of your ads and campaigns can help raise your position and, hopefully, your results.

Quality score

Quality score is the way Google ranks the quality of your keywords, ads, and landing pages. *This is discussed in-depth in Chapter 8.* The main points to remember about your quality score is that it changes frequently in relation to the performance of your keywords, ads, and landing pages. According to Google, "In general, the higher your quality score, the lower your costs and the better your ad position." Based on this, a high quality score is an important component to the success of your AdWords ads and campaigns.

First page bid estimates

This metric appears on your keyword analysis page and gives you an approximation of the CPC, cost-per-click, bid that you need for your ad to appear on the first page of a Google's search results. This bid amount combines with your quality score, your budget, account settings, and the way Google users behave. Because there are so many factors at place in having your ad appear on the first page of search results, meeting this bid amount does not guarantee its placement on the first page, but it can help you budget and give you an idea of what your competition is bidding to arrive there.

Position preference

AdWords allows you to let Google know where you want your ad to appear on a search results page if it is triggered by a keyword search. Please note that just because you specify a position preference, it does not mean you will get it, but you can request your ad not be shown lower than a given position, higher than a given position, in a single exact position, or within a range of positions.

Reporting options

With some advertising, marketing, and public relations efforts, it can be difficult or costly to determine effectiveness. With all of these efforts, tracking is crucial.

AdWords tracks results for you. And, you can customize how you see these results. The "reporting" tab is the place to go for this information. Once you get there, you can:

- Create a new report.
- View recently created reports (up to the last 15 you have created).
- View your report templates.

The reporting function of AdWords gives you numbers you need to determine what works and what needs to be tweaked. The reporting function lets you see:

- your impressions, or how often your ads are shown

- your clicks, or how many times someone clicked on your ad

- your CPC, or how much it cost you every time someone clicked on your ad

- your CTR, or click-through rates of your ads and keywords

- your conversions, or numbers of how many people clicked on an ad compared to those that did what you wanted them do, such as buy your product, fill out a survey, or leave their information so you can contact them later

No matter what type of ad you are using, including text, image, video, mobile, and local business ads, AdWords tracks the numbers for you. It also tracks this information for each of your keywords. This information makes it possible for you to determine if a specific keyword is most successful in a text ad versus an image ad. Based on the information about that keyword and that ad, you can decide if you should create more text ads or more image ads and continually hone your ads and campaigns to increase their success, increase your ROI, and increase your organization's success.

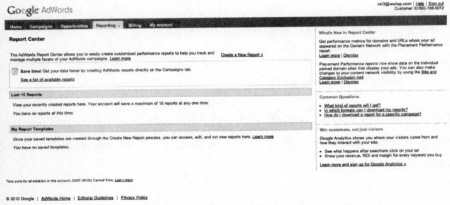

Google screenshots © Google Inc. Used with permission.

Click on the "create a new report" link to get started with your reporting. Several report types are available, and a brief summary of each is below:

- Placement / keyword performance: focuses on keywords or placements that you have specifically targeted

- Ad performance: shows data for each of your ads

- URL performance: focuses on your destination URLs and how each performs

- Ad group performance: gives performance data at the ad group level for one or more of your campaigns

- Campaign performance: gives performance data for your campaigns

- Account performance: gives information on how your entire account is performing.

- Demographic performance: allows you to view performance data by demographic.

- Geographic performance: focuses on geographic origin performance data.

- Search query performance: view which search queries triggered your ad and received clicks.

- Placement performance: used with Content Network sites, shows your ad's performance on sites where your ad has been shown

You can set your reports to view them by units of time, date ranges, and by different campaigns and ad groups. You can also add and remove columns in your reports and focus on campaigns, ad groups, or keywords. Information you can include in your customized reports can include keyword matching, quality score, daily budget, highest position preference, lowest position preference, ad group status, keyword status, campaign status, ad distribution, current maximum CPC, and keyword destination URL. Performance statistics options include impressions, clicks, click-through rate, average CPC, cost, and average position. Local business ad interaction columns may also be included, allowing you to see information on how users interact with the local business ads that you have included on Google Maps. You can see how many users open your info window from the left hand side and how many open it from the map marker. You can also see how many clicks you received from the "get directions" and "street view" options that Google Maps users have selected, and you can see how many users clicked to your website from the info window.

Results can by filtered by variety of options. This can be done under the "filter your results" hyperlink, which opens a pull-down menu that says, "show only keywords that match all of the following criteria …"

You can then select one, or several, filters that apply to your keywords. The filter options include: keyword, keyword matching, ad distribution, keyword status, ad group status, campaign status, impressions, clicks, CTR, average CPC, cost, and average position. These options can then be further sorted by status, amount, and other variables. You can also include keywords with zero impressions, so you can determine if there are ads in your Content Network campaigns that are not being shown at all, which can help you decide keyword effectiveness.

AdWords also includes some practical options for receiving your reports in the "create a report" section. You can name your report, set it as a new report template that allows you to use the same parameters without resetting them, and you can schedule the report to run automatically every day, every Monday, or on the first day of every month. You can also opt to have AdWords automatically send a notification e-mail to one or several e-mail addresses with or without an attachment of the report in the format that you choose. *More about your format options is in the upcoming section, Downloading Your Reports.*

If you do not want the report e-mailed to you, just leave the e-mail area blank. Also, if you selected the e-mail option and no longer want to receive notification via e-mail that the report has run, or if you want to change a recipient of the report, access the report center from the "reports" tab and follow these instructions:

1. Under "saved templates," locate the name of the scheduled report that you want to change and click "edit this template" next to its name.

2. On the "edit template" page, scroll down to "templates, scheduling and e-mail" at the bottom of the page and change the e-mail addresses or uncheck the box next to "whenever the report runs, send e-mail to ..."

3. Click "save template."

The only thing that changes about your report is the e-mail notification. The rest of your report template will run as your set up and scheduling options allow.

Analysis Tools to Help Your Bottom Line

Many analysis tools are available through AdWords and through Google's Business Solutions to help you determine what is working with your ads and campaigns, and what is not. Many other analysis tools available for Internet marketing campaigns may offer slightly different information or offer information in a way that is easier for you to understand and manage. Some of the analysis tools available include:

- *Reports*. AdWords reports and analytics are the key to the success of its advertisers, according to most of the AdWords users that provided the case studies found in this book. Reporting and analyzing the information from your ads, ad groups, and campaigns is the way you determine your ROI with AdWords. You can see the ROI that you receive from effectively managing your keywords and the rest of AdWords components in the many reports available to AdWords advertisers.

- *Analytics*. Google Analytics either works in conjunction with AdWords or independently to help you determine how many people found your site, and what they did when they arrived and traveled through your site. It also offers information on how to make their experience better next time they visit and, therefore, increase the productivity and results of your site. You can sign up for your Google Analytics account by going to **www.google.com/analytics/sign_up.html**

- *Diagnostic Tool.* Use this tool to help determine why your ad may not be appearing on the first page of search results for a specific keyword.

- *Hypertracker.net.* This site offers a tracking tools system that you can implement into any Internet marketing campaign. It analyzes sales and other actions on your site and provides campaign analysis.

- *AdGooroo* offers products and reports that include activity for Google, Yahoo®, MSN®, and Baidu for search engine marketers. Its site, **www.adgooroo.com**, can give you more information.

- *Wordtracker* uses a research tool for keyword research. For more information, check out its site at **www.wordtracker.com**.

- *KeywordSpy™.* At **www.keywordspy.com**, you can sign up for services that let you know who your competitors are, what keywords they are using, monitor and track keyword performance, and launch an affiliate campaign.

- *KeyCompete* offers an online keyword research tool that identifies the keywords your competitors are using and identifies your competition for keywords you are bidding on. Go to **www.keycompete.com** for more information.

- *Traffic Estimator* is a Google tool you can use to estimate search volume, average cost-per-click, ad positions, and keyword state for your keywords before you add them to an existing ad group or after you select the ones that you want to add. Find this tool at **https:// adwords.google.com/select/TrafficEstimatorSandbox**.

Downloading Your Reports

You can view your reports in your AdWords account, and you can also download them so you can do different types of comparisons, provide a printed report to a client or your boss, or to review it if you will not have access to AdWords online. You can use five formats to download your reports:

- .csv — for Excel®
- .csv — with comma-separated values
- .tsv — with tab-separated values
- .xml — extensible markup language
- .html — hypertext markup language

Knowing how you will use your report will help determine when to use each of these types of downloadable reports:

- .csv for Excel® is a report format compatible with most versions of Microsoft® Excel®. These files are encoded in UTF-16LE for older versions of Excel® and UTF-8 for more recent versions.

- .csv (comma-separated values) is a type of format that is organized by commas. A comma separates each value (in this case number), and then, the next value appears like this: emporium, hotcakes, 53. Use this format to review your information in a text-only format. It can also be used with Excel® and may be your format of choice if your file is very large. This format is encoded in UTF-8.

- .tsv (tab-separated values) is much like .csv. Use it if you want to review your information in a text-only format. The difference is that tabs, instead of commas, divide the information. The format is encoded in UTF-8 and can be used with Excel®.

- .xml (extensible markup language) gives you more precision in your results because it lists values in millionths of a unit and is the only format you can use if your report is more than 100 megabytes (MB) in size. A report this large would include an enormous amount of information and should probably be divided by date ranges or keywords to give you more manageable information. This format is Web-friendly and can be used to publish data in multiple formats.

- .html (hypertext markup language) allows you to view your report as a Web page. This makes sharing remotely via the Web easier.

Before you download reports, ask your IT professional which of these is most compatible with software that you have available. If you are a small business and do not have an IT professional on hand, Excel® spreadsheets can be challenging to manipulate if you are familiar with the program, but it does not have a huge learning curve for simple reporting needs, and it can sort and make graphs for easier understanding.

A/B split testing

An A/B split test is a common way that AdWords users can test the performance of two or more versions (one A and one B) of the same ad or landing page. Doing this helps you determine which is most effective so you can focus your efforts and budget on the one or ones, that are most successful for you. Split tests are typically run to determine the highest CTR, or click-through rate, but can also be used to determine ROI, branding, and clarity.

CASE STUDY: TAKE A LOOK AT THE NUMBERS

G.1440
2031 Clipper Park Road, Suite 105,
Baltimore, MD 21211
www.g1440.com
tkassouf@g1440.com
(410) 843-3800
(410) 843-3853 fax
Tim Kassouf - Director of Marketing

CLASSIFIED CASE STUDIES™
directly from the experts

G.1440 offers IT staffing services and IT consulting solutions including search engine optimization, business analysis and IT strategy, website design, and custom IT application development. It is a full-service design, development, and online marketing shop that uses AdWords to promote print and online subscriptions for a prominent local newspaper.

The campaign for this case study is specifically designed to reach buyers, not just to generate Web traffic. The budget for this campaign is about $1,500 per month. The keywords used are all designed to be what users would search for if looking for a news source, either by name or generally (e.g. the Washington Post versus "newspaper"). Subscriptions currently fall into two categories, print subscriptions and online subscriptions. The ad text generally uses variable keywords, and the ads are written specifically for the associated keyword groups. This means that while G.1440 did not have to manage an infinite number of ads for this campaign, ads can still be delivered that make sense and that feature the keyword or phrase that was actually searched.

Maximizing bids for this campaign was important, and G.1440 did this to get the highest placements possible. G.1440 also designed its ad copy to eliminate unwanted clicks by including very specific selling information. For example, rather than messaging that is focused on the value of the newspaper alone, such as "This is the best news source ever," it uses messaging that touches on value, but that is also specific about an action, such as "Subscribe to the area's top news source at our lowest rate ever — Today only."

In this campaign, G.1440 has learned that its particular target audience responds to a total price better than a smaller monthly price. "We thought it would be the other way around," director of marketing Tim Kassouf said. "But, $60 per year (subscribers get a discount for paying up front) got a better response than $7 per month."

G.1440 took over managing this campaign from another company and after the first month, the client wanted to know why the total clicks were down. G.1440's strategy was to pay for buyers, not just traffic, and crafted the ads to be unappealing to casual browsers. They then pointed the client to the sales results. The previous company had shown one conversion in six months and G.1440 had more 20 in the first month. The client has not questioned G.1440 about these numbers again.

Between 500 and 1,000 clicks per month typically are generated from this campaign, and conversions are averaging about 20 to 30 per month. Each subscription purchase is worth about $200 per year, and, on average, G.1440 gives a more than $3,000 return on the client's $1,500 budget.

Interestingly, G.1440 dedicates 20 percent of its monthly total budget to trying something new and different. "Because we run controlled experiments, we are looking for a specific result, and we are able to use analytics to determine if a test was successful and should be expanded," Kassouf said.

HOT TIPS from Kassouf:

- Strategy and testing are so important. Make sure your campaign is built toward achieving the goals that make sense, and that you are monitoring and testing it. You can spend thousands and thousands of dollars on clicks, and it is easy to get addicted to that traffic, but if it is not helping you achieve your goals, it is a waste.

- Create appropriate groupings so every individual user has a logical experience from search to ad to landing page.

- Analytics are everything. Use them for testing, and study your results to determine what works and what does not.

HOT TIP: Focus on one variable, such as ad text, for each split test, and make it different. Your results will give you more focused information on that variable.

To run a split test, create a new ad within your campaign, or start a new campaign. Google runs ads equally within a single campaign, so you can compare the results more accurately. As you see results, continue to tweak your ads, and run more split tests to optimize your campaigns.

Explore new products and services inexpensively

Developing a new product, or offering a new service, can be an enormous investment. Besides the expenditures of manufacturing or assembling a new product, employee training, advertising, budgeting, and distribution can quickly swell costs. That is why product testing is important. Before jumping into a new product, service, or entirely new business venture, it is prudent to test the market. Google AdWords can help you do that quickly, and on your budget terms, by allowing you to run a few test ads, measure their response, and stop the ads when your budget limit is reached.

Prototypes, product testing, consumer surveys and polls, direct mail, and telephone market research are costly and time consuming. If done properly, they are worth the time and energy because they can give you crucial feedback to influence costly decisions you will make about your new product or service.

You can integrate Google AdWords easily into a comprehensive market research plan. It also may be useful as an initial testing ground to influence the direction and scope of other market research. For example, say your family and friends love your hotcakes. They have encouraged you for years to open your own hotcakes restaurant. Before you quit your day job, knock a wall out in your kitchen, and install a gigantic hotcakes oven, you could test this idea with Google AdWords.

There are a number of ways you could use AdWords to predetermine the viability of your hotcakes business venture. Please note that with any advertising or product testing, do not say you will do something you have no intention of doing. As you do testing, explain to potential customers that you are in the pre-launch or testing phase. Offer them a free sample if you have them and are willing to take the time and expense to ship the samples in a timely manner. You could also offer a discounted rate for those who sign up for your mailing list. At this point, your aim is to collect and analyze information, not to actually provide the product. Make that clear on your landing page, which customers see after they click on your ad.

Also, with any testing, keep in mind that all the tests should be equitable in as many components as possible. If one ad runs twice as much as another ad, any comparisons and conclusions you make from the test results will be faulty. It is important to be consistent, and, in this case, compare hotcakes to hotcakes. Keep all of the components of your ad the same except for the component you are testing. The changed component is your test item, in this case, your hotcakes. In this example, to test the popularity of different hotcake flavors, the only component you would change would be the name of the flavor. Everything else about the ads would be the same. As you test, factor in the unknown. If you do not yet know which times or sites produce the most click-throughs, and, therefore, the most information, run the test ads simultaneously. Once you determine that one factor receives a better response than another, include the more popular factor in all of your other tests. With your hotcakes, if you determine that blueberry is the flavor that receives a better response, use it. Knowing that blueberry hotcakes are the most popular gives you an added boost when you use it.

As you whittle and hone your ads and campaigns this way, use the best options from each test to get the best result.

Using percentages in marketing research is key, but make sure to keep them within the perspective of your overall market. With the hotcakes example, if you get ten responses to your ads for powdered mixes, and three of those expressed a similar preference by responding to the blueberry ad, it is accurate to say that 30 percent of your respondents favor the blueberry option over the other flavor options. Keep in mind that being accurate and being realistic are not always the same.

If you realistically anticipate 100,000 responses to an ad or campaign, your test size should mirror the size of your desired response. When testing, be sure to consider your sample size, or your response numbers, in context with the decision you are making. The bigger the sample size, the better your results will be. So, in testing, be patient so that the analysis that AdWords provides to you is on a realistic scale with the result you are anticipating. It will provide response information about ads you have run as your test. You will need to calculate the percentages to compare your test, or sample, with your expected results.

With these points as a foundation for your testing, look at information options that Google AdWords can provide, using your hotcakes business example. This is a hypothetical example, but if you were doing this as a real test, you must not offer something to potential customers that you are not able to deliver.

- If you promise a free sample as an enticement in your ad, be prepared to send a free sample. In this case, you could prepare bags of your powdered mix to give as a free sample.

- You could also promise customers a discount on their first order if they add their name and e-mail address to your potential customer database. You would customize the ad and the offer to whatever works with your product or service, and make certain you are prepared to follow up with the sample or the discount, or whatever you choose as the enticement in your ad.

Name testing

You like the name Hotcake Emporium for the name of your possible business venture. Your best friend feels strongly, however, that Adventures in Hotcakes is the name you should use. Other suggestions you are considering include: The Hotcake Outlet, to appeal to more price conscious consumers; World's Best Hotcakes, for a higher-quality appeal; and Hotcakes by Grandma, to give the business a homespun feel.

With Google AdWords, you can test them all quickly and inexpensively. You can write the same ad and include different names, running them each for the same amount of time. In this case, running the ads simultaneously should give you results that are more realistic because you are testing the response to a perception, or an idea, rather than a specific product. You would run five separate ads, each written the same, but using a different name for your business. This allows you to test the effectiveness of each of your five name ideas with the same number and types of users. At this point in your pre-launch research, you are searching for the name that potential customers respond to most frequently. If the response to Hotcake Emporium receives a higher percentage of click-throughs than all of the other options combined, that is the name you should probably use. However, if the results are similar, you can now make an informed decision on your new business name, based on test results that indicate the name of the business is not a deciding factor for those who want fluffy, fried hotcakes delivered to their door.

Market testing

You now need to find out who is most likely to order your hotcakes online, so do an assessment of who likes to eat them the most. Your children love them, but prefer them to be in fun shapes, such as in their initials. The local firefighters and police rave about them every year when you deliver them as a holiday gift from your family. Everyone at your church insists you act as hotcake chef during their annual fund-raising breakfast; you do not know if this is a compliment to you or a way for them to get out of cooking.

The problem is that you know all of these people, and they know you and live near you. Though you are able to gather results based on these people, it is important to extend your research beyond those who know you and may be biased. With Google AdWords, there is a way to test various markets and determine which is the most profitable. You can test worldwide, nationally, regionally, within your state, or you can keep it local.

An important part of marketing your product, the hotcakes, is to cater your sales approach to a particular audience, or in this case, to a variety of different audiences. Be creative in using ways to present your product or service to meet the needs of your potential customers. For kids, how about a giant birthday hotcake customized with their initials, plus little ones for their guests? How about including your powdered mix in corporate gift baskets? How about providing the mix or frozen version to nonprofits for a fund-raising opportunity? These may all be far-fetched, but you can use AdWords to find success by testing all of these options simultaneously and adjusting each campaign based on its results. If none of the campaigns significantly increase orders, just advertise within your local geographic area to those already familiar with your yummy bread product. If one or all of these markets prove to be profitable, you can use the money to test other markets, invest in a new stove, or hire someone to clean your kitchen.

Specific product testing

Your fund-raising, gift basket, and birthday hotcake markets are all grow-ing exponentially and your customers have started making requests for spe-cialty hotcakes in flavors such as blueberry, cinnamon, and chocolate chip. The additional ingredients in these make them more expensive and you would like to buy separate mixers for each flavor so you can mix them si-multaneously. How do you determine which flavors you should include in your standard flavor options? You guessed it — test them all through sepa-rate AdWords campaigns. With AdWords, you could also offer seasonal flavors, such as pumpkin, and test name options such as Plump Pumpkin or Harvest Hotcakes. In this case, you would run separate ads, worded the same, except for the specialty flavors. Again, you should be prepared to deliver what you offer, so if you are providing these flavors to fill additional customer requests, mix up a little extra so you can send the mix to those responding to your ad. If you are doing a limited campaign for testing purposes, you could limit your ads to what you can actually fulfill. In the case of our Hotcakes examples, you would run the ad that has proven to be most successful for you to test the popularity of new flavors. In the ad, you would include the hotcake flavor. So, if you would like to test three flavors, you would run an ad for each flavor. You would only insert the name of one flavor in each of the three ads so you would end up with a blueberry ad, a cinnamon ad, and a chocolate chip ad.

When you compare your response rate (which equals potential sales) with your cost to buy a new mixer plus the additional ingredients, you can de-termine if your sales will pay for the additional cost, plus continue to make money for your business. AdWords makes it easy and inexpensive to give potential customers a choice and let them determine, based on response, if it would be profitable. When you can respond to the needs of your customers quickly and consistently, they are more likely to become repeat customers and give you the added benefit of word-of-mouth advertising.

Alternative product options

Separate ads run simultaneously on AdWords can measure initial consumer response. The same ad, with different landing pages, can also provide you with valuable information. Using this second option, you know that your ad is getting a response because people are clicking on it. Once you get them to the landing page, their response, whether it be placing an order, offering their address, or closing your page, AdWords analytical tools will tell you if the frozen hotcake landing page or the powdered mix landing page actually gave you more customers.

You are getting some positive feedback about your idea to open a restaurant and to sell hotcakes online and ship them all over the world. Now you need to consider packaging options. Do your potential customers respond more positively to your idea of shipping frozen hotcakes? Or, do they prefer the secret family recipe, hotcake powdered mix delivered to their door? In this case, you could run two ads. They would be worded the same, except that they would include the delivery option as the only difference in the ads. Another way you could test this is to run the same ad, but with different destination URLs, which take "ad clickers" to different landing pages. If you did this, you would send some potential customers to a landing page that offers frozen hotcakes, and you would send other potential customers to a landing page that offers powdered mix. In this situation, you would determine your option based on the conversion rate (how many ad clicks turn into customers) from your landing pages. Again, be prepared to ship some frozen hotcakes and some powdered mix. This is also a great way to get customer feedback. Let customers know they are getting a discount for helping you test these options, and then include them on a list to target once you determine which option makes customers the happiest, and costs you less.

Time testing

Hotcakes are traditionally thought of as a breakfast food, so use AdWords to schedule your hotcake ads to run during particular hours of the day and on specific days of the week. You could run a campaign for a few weeks, or a single week, and then run an hourly report to determine if consumers are more likely to come to your restaurant or order hotcakes during specific times or on specific days. The hourly report does not have to be run every hour. But rather, it tells you which times of the day your ad is clicked on.

What works for me?

Businesses of every size make AdWords work for them everyday. If they can do it, you can do it. The key to analyzing AdWords, and any other marketing, advertising, or promotions campaign, is to make it work within your budget and to get the return that you need from your investment. To determine most effectively if the results are working for you, you must know the following:

- What is the amount of my investment?
- What is the return on my investment that I need to make this worth the effort?
- What can I do differently to improve my existing ads?
- What can I do differently to improve my existing campaigns?

Remember to factor in some time and expense for a learning curve, since making mistakes and then making your AdWords campaign better is part of the process.

Chapter Eleven

Maintaining a Profitable Presence within Google Business Solutions

In advertising, marketing, and public relations, reaching the target audience to share the message that is most pertinent to them is the name of the game. Getting your message across effectively to your target audience in any campaign means offering that message in as many places as possible that your target audience might frequent. This is no different when using Google's Business Solutions. The more far-reaching the campaign, the more likely your target is to see it and respond to it. Sometimes nooks, crannies or venues that are not initially obvious to you are the places that bring out a surprising number of respondents. Many of the case studies featured in this book mention that using AdWords gave them benefits they did not expect, such as new distribution channels.

With AdWords, you can jump in immediately to all the different ad formats and options offered. Keywords are the driving force of all of Google's Business Solution options. The same keywords will work with many different campaigns and types of ads. But, if you start slowly with AdWords text ads and use the experience you gain, and the information that Google's analysis solutions provides, your other ventures will probably be easier to conceptualize, develop, and manage. They will also probably be more profitable because you will be savvier about keyword effectiveness, bidding, and conversions.

Working with Google Business Solutions

As you are now aware, AdWords is more than simple text ads running down the side of a search page. In developing the AdWords system, Google has also developed companion products for business owners to drive traffic to its search engine and make your business or organization a relevant stop on the Web.

Using Google Search on your website

With Google Search, you put a Google search box on your website so that visitors can stay on your site to search the Web. Instead of opening another browser window to activate a Google search, users can do it within your page. Search result pages are displayed on your site, and just as the advertiser pays Google if a user clicks on an ad, Google pays you, the site's publisher, for the click.

As a website publisher, Google Search can benefit you because it allows users to search both your site and the Web. This allows customers to find what they are looking for on your site, whether it is content or product information, making your site user friendly, accommodating, and engaging. When users find the product they are searching for, they are more likely to buy it.

As with AdSense, Google Search allows you, as the website's publisher, to control the look and feel of the search box as it appears on your site. You can also quickly and easily customize the look of the search results pages that appear on your site. You can choose from more than 200 colors for the title, text, background, URL, and other features. You can also add your company logo.

To help you build and maintain your site in response to your visitors' behavior, Google allows you to see what your users are looking for. As users search your site through your customized search box, Google compiles a list of the information they search for and creates a "top queries" report. The report includes the 25 most common searches on your site. This information, as well as the number of queries, clicks, and your click-through rate, can be tracked through the same account that you use to track your AdSense earnings.

The same criteria Google uses to review ads that appears on its own search pages, and through the AdSense program, is used to ensure the ads that appear on your site's search pages are suitable for all audiences. You can also block ads from competitors and other specific URLs from appearing on your site's search results pages.

You can apply for Google Search when you apply for AdSense.

Using AdSense

If you have a website, you can earn money through the Google AdSense program. Sign-up is free and Google only places relevant ads on your site. Users of AdWords provide the ads that appear on websites. You control the look, feel, and placement of the ads so that they integrate seamlessly within your site.

AdSense gives you four options for ad placement. They are:

- ads on your website's content pages

- ads on search page results within your website

- ads for mobile users, which include cell phones and multi-function phones, such as the Blackberry® and iPhone®

- ads within the content of your RSS feed, which sends updated content to those who request it from you

Through AdSense, ads may appear on the content pages of your website. For example, if your website focuses on nutrition, an ad for a new hotcakes business would correspond nicely because of the all-natural ingredients in the hotcakes.

Through the AdSense program, website publishers may also include a Google search engine to search within their site, or search the Web through your site. Because Google's primary function is as a search engine, this gives you the ability to offer yet another solution through your website for your site's visitors. You can create a customized search engine that offers ads on the search results pages. You earn money when ads that appear on your search page are clicked. You can fine-tune your search results and the ads that show on the results pages to match with the interests of your site's visitors, or to match your site's content.

Searches for information through Google take place in businesses, in homes, in airports, or wherever there are people with access to a computer. They also take place in cars, on sidewalks, in waiting rooms, and wherever there are people with access to a cell phone. Because information is now mobile, Google offers advertising through your mobile Web pages. Mobile Web pages include reformatted text, resized images, and, in the case of AdSense, specially formatted text and image ads.

With AdSense, you can also earn revenue through your RSS feed, which is information you publish and provide to anyone who wants it. As with the mobile AdSense option, appropriately targeted text and image ads are displayed along with the content of your RSS feed.

Ad Planner

Ad Planner is a free media-planning tool offered by Google. With it, you can build a media plan and identify websites your target customers are likely to visit. It helps you first define your audience and categorize it by interests and demographics. You can then use your audience's demographic information to search for websites that your target audience might be using. The data that this tool provides for millions of websites all over the world allows you to analyze websites by page views, unique users, and more. All of this information helps you build a media plan.

This tool makes data available and then easily walks you through creation of a media plan. You can add sites automatically or manually to your media plan, and you can develop plans for yourself or for your clients. This can help you determine which sites are relevant for advertising on the Content Network and which sites may not be the most effective in delivering members of your target audience to your site.

For those with a website, the Ad Planner tool allows you to manage the information that appears in Ad Planner about your site. This helps you market your site to advertisers, helps them search for you, and helps you provide the most accurate numbers for your site. For more information on Ad Planner, go to **www.google.com/adplanner**.

CASE STUDY:
MAKING ADWORDS WORK
FOR THE CLIENT

eZanga
222 Carter Drive Suite 201,
Middletown, DE 19709
www.ezanga.com
webmaster@eZanga.com
(888) 4-EZANGA

Based in Delaware, eZanga provides online advertisers with local, regional, and national advertising focused on generating a high return on investment. EZanga offers SEM, PPC, and contextual advertising solutions. EZanga also operates a search engine, which is powered by proprietary technologies that take advantage of metasearch by retrieving search results from multiple search engines and re-ranking and displaying the most relevant results without duplication. EZanga was deemed Delaware's fastest growing company by Inc. magazine in 2008.

When an eZanga client, Bedco Mobility, was established in 1912, it was one of the first companies to identify the need for equipment servicing the disabled. After being in business for almost 100 years, Bedco has become a national leader within the accessibility industry, making the company the specialists of mobility equipment requiring both service and installation.

Bedco supplies and installs quality stair lifts, wheelchair lifts, and handicap automotive products, such as ramped minivans, wheelchair lifts, scooter lifts, and driving aids. It is considered the "one-stop shop" for all accessibility needs, reinforcing the company's motto, "The Total Access Company."

Although it was an established company, Bedco Mobility exclusively advertised in local newspapers and yellow pages with no online representation other than its website. After concluding it needed a more innovative approach to reach its target audience, Bedco Mobility implemented eZanga's SEM service to enhance exposure and profitability.

Bedco's major objective was to increase leads and spread positive regional brand awareness, while also drawing a specifically targeted audience to its reliable products and services. eZanga built, implemented, and optimized Bedco's advertising campaign which included:

- creation of the keyword listings and ad

- targeting Bedco's ad to a refined local audience to produce the most leads within the service area

- placing the campaign on all major search engines including Google, Yahoo!®, and MSN®

- monitoring and tracking all telephone and e-mail inquiries.

EZanga adjusted the campaign frequently based on reports and analysis. Bedco's online inquiries were infrequent before eZanga implemented its online advertising service. With the same budget, eZanga has more than doubled Bedco's online inquiries within a four-month period.

Lead generation increased dramatically with:

- a 38.7 percent increase in month two, compared to month one

- a 58 percent increase in month three, compared to month one

- a 135.5 percent increase in month four, compared to month one

EZanga's unique service uses phone call tracking and optimizations so that if a Google user does a search, your ad appears; the user clicks on your ad and uses the phone number on your site to call you to place their order, and the phone call is tracked. With Google's Analytics, this scenario shows as a non-conversion. The conversion here took place over the phone rather than via a website.

HOT TIPS from eZanga:

- Tailor your AdWords campaign to work for you or your client.

- AdWords can expand your advertising efforts through targeted keywords, ads, and audiences.

Web resources for starting and maintaining campaigns for you

AWeber is an e-mail marketing provider that provides e-mail marketing tools, including e-mail newsletters, autoresponders, and RSS to e-mail. For more information on the company's services and pricing, go to **www.awe-ber.com**.

- G.1440 offers IT consulting solutions including website design, SEO services, business analysis and IT strategy, custom IT application development, as well as providing IT staffing services. For more information on what G.1440 can do for your business, go to www.g1440.com. *A case study from G.1440 appears in Chapter 9.*

- HubSpot offers inbound marketing software that helps small- and medium-sized business get found on the Internet by qualified prospects through managing search engines, blogs and the blogosphere, and social media, and converting them through landing pages, lead intelligence, and marketing analytics. For more information on HubSpot's offerings, go to **www.hubspot.com**.

Supervising an agency that operates these services for you

Time is often the enemy of marketing and advertising professionals. It is a deadline-driven industry that seems to be consistently accelerating its pace through the capability of "instant marketing" via social media outlets such as Twitter, Facebook, LinkedIn®, and others. But, the flip side of the fast-paced world of marketing is that there are marketing, advertising, and public relations professionals who do all of this everyday and can do it quickly, efficiently, and professionally with you, or for you. Now that you are armed with the knowledge of how Google's Business Solutions work, you are much more prepared to oversee an agency, freelancer, or even a department or personnel within your own company who can handle your AdWords campaigns for you.

Just as you would go through the processes of exploring your business, its current market status, and your competitors (*as we did in the "In the Beginning" section of this book*), anyone handling your AdWords campaigns, or any other promotional work for your company, should ask questions before they do anything else. Use the guides, worksheets, and quizzes throughout this book to anticipate and answer their questions truthfully and fully. The more information they are armed with, the more effective they can be in operating promotional activities for you. If they are not asking questions similar to those we have covered that are necessary in understanding your business, your customers, and your operations, they may not be qualified or fully equipped with the correct information to operate successful, results-driven campaigns on your behalf.

Once they complete their information-gathering phase, you should be prepared to approve anything they plan to launch before your target audience sees it. This should be done, especially at first, to ensure that your company's image is consistently portrayed in everything it does. Even after a level of trust has been established between your company and your new marketing "partner," client approval is standard procedure and should never be taken for granted.

With approvals on materials produced by someone else for you, be considerate. Agencies and individuals are typically juggling work for other clients in addition to their work for you, and hold-ups on approvals and re-dos can be costly and quickly move your account into the "not worth the hassle" category of their clients. You should, in turn, expect consideration of your time and other obligations. Instant approval requests should be rare and may indicate a lack of planning on their part. Communicating deadlines in advance will help both of you handle the time management of your campaigns and ensure that you take full advantage of placements and timing issues that may affect your promotional efforts.

Once your campaign is launched, expect to see results. A huge component of planning and preparation for your campaign should be in setting measurable goals and objectives for each campaign. You now know that with AdWords, and every other advertising venue we could list, a number of factors should be considered in reaching your target audience. Expect to set realistic goals you can measure, so you can work together on long-range planning, including expectations for future and current campaigns.

The results you get from your AdWords campaign should be clear and easy to understand. You are now aware of multiple analytical tools offered through Google, and the job of someone handling your campaigns should be to provide results to your specifications. If you do not want details of every ad, or of every campaign, request summaries instead. Be prepared to discuss the results and your ROI from each campaign to help create campaigns that continually increase your response rates.

It is also important to note that when you can view an outside agency or freelancer as part of the internal workings of your organization, you can most effectively work with them to anticipate issues and changes in the marketplace that may affect your campaign results. For example, if you are considering a new product launch, include them in the planning of the marketing materials and launch calendar. Not only will their expertise in presentations be beneficial, but it also will work in your favor when they are prepared to launch your AdWords campaign as part of your overall launch strategy.

Worksheet: Imagine You are the Customer

Whether you are handling your AdWords campaigns yourself, or supervising an agency or individual who does it for you, at some point in your planning process of a successful AdWords campaign, you have to put yourself in the mind of your customer or target audience. These questions also apply to any marketing, advertising, or public relations campaign you undertake, because your goal is to think the way they do so you can most effectively reach them with your message. Here are some questions to ask to help you think the way your target audience thinks.

1. What are the top three features, or characteristics of my product or service that my target audience responds to?

    a.

    b.

    c.

2. What are the benefits of each of those top three features, or characteristics?

    Feature #1:

    a.

    b.

    c.

    Feature #2:

    a.

    b.

    c.

    Feature #3:

    a.

    b.

    c.

3. Now, under each benefit you listed in question two above, write down the message that will most effectively communicate to your target audience. To do this, pretend that you are a member of your target audience, and use the question, "What will this do for me, and how can it affect my life to help me?"

Chapter Twelve

How do I Make the System Work Better?

Google is constantly changing its AdWords product. Your business or organization is also probably changing constantly, and your AdWords efforts can easily change as well. Using the analytics portion of AdWords can help you continue to change for the better, and this chapter focuses on tips and techniques for constantly improving your AdWords ROI.

CASE STUDY:
CHECK YOUR NUMBERS
AGAINST YOUR RESULTS

Pacific Prime
Unit 1-11, 35th Floor, One Hungto
Road, Kwun Tong, Hong Kong
www.pacificprime.com
Michael@kwiksure.com
(866) 383-0456
Michael Lamb — Web Development
Manager

Pacific Prime Insurance Brokers Ltd. offers professional advice on family, individual, group, travel, and teacher expatriate health insurance. It promotes its international health Insurance product through AdWords. This product is needed mostly by expatriates, or individuals who are currently living outside of their home country and is fundamentally different from local or national health insurance.

The goal of this campaign is to direct users to the website, where they are asked to complete a form containing their details. This information is then placed in a client database and followed up on by a client executive. "By imbedding the code provided by AdWords into your site, you can track users through to their conversions," said Michael Lamb, Web development manager at Pacific Prime. "There are better tools available, but the AdWords code is simple to use and incredibly easy to set up. Using the AdWords tracking code in conjunction with Google Analytics and Google Webmaster Tools will help you generate a very good overall assessment for the performance of your site and your AdWords account."

An average international health insurance policy offered by Pacific Prime would cost approximately $5,000 per year. Lamb's analysis shows that up to 25 percent of those who request more information will ultimately purchase a policy. Every person who responds to the Pacific Prime AdWords ad and requests information is counted as an "action." And, according to Lamb, "the most accurate figure that you can use to gain the 'health' of an account is cost per action (CPA). Current CPA for my accounts varies from $15 to 20. We can reasonably assume a conservative 25 percent success rate in sales against all conversions. Out of 100 leads with a CPA of $15, for a total cost of $1,500, we can expect to gain an estimated $125,000 in policy premiums. As you can see, the ROI is well in excess of 100 percent."

Lamb learned through some surprising numbers that your AdWords results should be compared to the results you see in other parts of your business. "I had an AdWords account that was consistently outperforming all my others when it came to the total number of conversions on the site at a rate of 40 percent conversions compared to the typical 20 percent," he said. "When I investigated to determine what was making this account so special, I noticed that the conversions I had been getting were not being mirrored in my client database. There just were not as many new leads as there should have been, and the account CTR and traffic was no better than any of my other leads. I eventually discovered my conversion code snippet had been duplicated on the site on pages that had no relevance to the lead generation. AdWords was telling me that users browsing the site were converting. I removed the duplicated code form the non-relevant pages and learned my lesson: Never make assumptions, and if something looks off, it probably is."

HOT TIPS from Lamb:

- Improve your AdWords (and consequently your quality score) by focusing on four areas: the campaign, the ad groups, keywords, and ad text.

- Make sure each ad group is specific to a unique theme. Save yourself the trouble of dissecting and dividing massive lists of keywords at a later date by organizing your campaign into coherent, logical themes. It really helps the maintenance of your account.

- Check, check, and check again. AdWords is not infallible, and if you make a mistake with something like the conversion code, you are setting yourself up for bad data.

Google AdWords Possibilities

AdWords opens up quite a few possibilities for your business or organization that you may have thought were unlikely before. It makes Internet advertising simple, which makes reaching potential customers fairly simple. It also makes it possible to gather information from potential customers that you might not otherwise reach to help fuel your efforts and ultimately, fund them. Increased profitability can be the result of your AdWords advertising and information-gathering efforts.

Google reported earnings of nearly $22 billion in 2008. Google's advertising revenues made up 97 percent of that amount. Google reports that worldwide use of its AdWords and AdSense programs includes hundreds of thousands of advertisers and partners. Why would so many businesses use this medium? Because they are making money.

In a free market economy, what does not work disappears. Since 2000, the AdWords program has grown from 350 advertisers to hundreds of thousands, and counting. Something good must be happening to perpetuate this rate of growth, and it is possible for you to easily add yourself to the number of advertisers profiting from the AdWords program.

All of the advertisers using Google's Business Solutions are not huge conglomerates with unlimited advertising budgets. But, the combined revenue from the big guys and lots and lots of little guys equals big dollars for Google. It can also equal big dollars for anyone willing to make an investment of their time and money into growing their business or organization through the easy-to-use AdWords program.

The entire goal of advertising is to effect a change in the behavior of the target audience. Behavioral changes can come in the form of purchasing a new product, donating to a charity, using a different service, supporting a candidate for political office, acting on behalf of a worthy cause, and responding to the pleas of your child to give them money for a new video game. Advertising has a lot of layers, and it can affect behavioral change without initially reaching the decision maker.

Decision makers — the individuals or groups who ultimately have the power to make a final purchasing or usage decision — are optimal targets for advertising, but secondary targets, such as those who influence the decision makers, should not be forgotten. In our video-game example, the child does not have the money to buy the video game and is not the decision maker, but, the influence that the child has on the parent that makes the buying decision is real and impactful. One of the benefits of Google AdWords is that you can target and reach a variety of audiences in a cost-effective way. Receiving the optimum benefit from your advertising dollars and getting the most from the time and energy you spend promoting your business is crucial to profitability.

CASE STUDY: NOT JUST SALES GAINED THROUGH ADWORDS

Apollo Nutrition, LLC
P.O. Box 803013
Dallas, TX 75380
www.drinkthc.com
(214) 485-0608
Anthony Adams — President

Apollo Nutrition sells an all-natural hangover prevention dietary supplement called The Hangover Cure at **www.drinkthc.com**. Most of its business is done online, and AdWords is its main source of advertising. Apollo Nutrition's AdWords effort is focused on one ongoing campaign that it has run for several months. The campaign includes several variations of the same ad.

"I spend about $25 a day on AdWords with an average PPC of $0.72," said Anthony Adams, president of Apollo Nutrition. "This ensures top placement most of the time as my competitors spend in the $0.50 range. I target keyword search terms, like 'hangover cure,' 'hangover drink,' 'buy hangover cure,' and 'best hangover cure.'"

The nature of the hangover cure product is such that there is not a lot of direct competition in AdWords. This helps keep the cost per click low, unlike many other more competitive terms for more competitive businesses that can run upwards of $20 per click. "It was very affordable to get started, and we felt the results the same day," said Adams. "For every $10 I spend on AdWords, I make $100 in sales, which is ten times the cost of advertising on a daily basis."

"AdWords, to me, is the most effective form of advertising on the planet. People are telling you exactly what they want, and anyone can compete by getting a chance to put their product in front of them," said Adams. "Nothing else compares, not even Facebook, which I recommend avoiding. The problem with Facebook ads, which are similar in structure to AdWords, is that they are still proactive, where as AdWords is reactive. People go on Facebook to find people, not products."

"With AdWords, our response results and our financial results improved. We have also found many of our independent distributors through AdWords. So, it is not just used as a sales tool, we also find interested business partners," said Adams.

HOT TIPS from Adams:

- If you are selling a product, be sure to include the price of your product and the word "buy" in your ad copy. Tell people what they are expected to do when they click on your site. This cuts down on errant clicks and saves you money.

- Do not trick anyone into going to your site. Do the opposite. Make your ads as unappealing as possible to anyone other than exactly who you are targeting to maximize your results. Tell them they will be expected to purchase your product. This cuts out anyone looking for a free sample or hand out. Go a step further by advertising a higher price in your AdWords copy than your product actually sells for. That way, you are bringing over-qualified visitors to your site.

In marketing, advertising, and public relations, knowing your target audience helps you spend money in the right places, reaching those most likely to respond to your efforts. With AdWords, targeting Internet users with savvy, relevant advertising makes reaching your profitability goals much easier. AdWords can help you increase revenue, and, more important, it can do it at a lower cost than many other advertising venues. It can also save money through saving time and the costs spent on printing mailers or filming television ads. Remember, **more money + more savings = more profitability**.

If your increased revenue is absorbed by increased cost in time and implementation, and you come closer to a break-even proposition, you are working for little or no benefit. For example, if your magazine advertisement brings in a lot of customers, that is great. But, if you make $2,500 on business from new customers that responded to your ad, and you spent $300 having someone design and create the ad, plus $2,000 for the cost of placing the ad, you have spent $2,300 on the ad and only made $2,500. In this case, you must consider if your time and energy was well spent for a $200 return. The cost of AdWords is totally determined by you. If you do not have the money to invest in a specific keyword bid, you can wait until next month or until you get the money to make the bid on the keyword you want.

Also, if you see that a campaign is not profitable, stop it, or change it. This is not as easy to do with other advertising media. For example, a business owner or marketing professional may schedule many direct mail campaigns and arrange for them to be staggered so the call center handling calls generated from the mailer will not be overwhelmed. If 100,000 mail pieces are printed, labeled, and prepared for mailing, only 25,000 would be mailed to homes on Monday of the first week. On Wednesday, another 25,000 would be mailed; the next Monday, the third batch of 25,000 would be mailed; the final 25,000 would be sent on the following Wednesday. This way, the call center could handle immediate responses without increased hold times for potential customers. This is a great way to handle large-quantity mailers; the call center is trained and prepared to handle calls pertaining to this special discounted offer. But sometimes the first wave of mailers does not generate a large response, and even the second batch may not increase calls significantly. At this point, do you scrap the last half of the printed, prepared mail pieces and swallow the cost of development, printing, and preparation? Or, do you send the remaining mailers at one time and hope that there is some response generated? With AdWords, the decision is easy: Go to the site, make a few changes to your ad, and start over. This can be done in a few minutes, with very little lost development cost. Printing, production, and mail-prep costs are not lost because they are never accrued.

Enhancement Extras

Once you have set your ad campaigns, you are well on your way to bringing customers to your business. But you may want to use a few other programs Google provides to enhance your ads and ensure that your ads are always top-notch.

Google Mobile and iGoogle

IGoogle is Google's version of a customized home page for Google users who have a sign-in account. Creating a sign-in account is easy.

Once your free sign-in account is created, you can customize your iGoogle page to include your Gmail messages and an amazing number of content options from the Web with Google Gadgets. Some of the basic options include weather, stock quotes, news headlines, sports news, movie showtimes, and quotes of the day. Besides customizing your iGoogle page's content, you can arrange the content so it appears in the order that you prefer. Once you set up your iGoogle page, you can switch to the Google Classic home page through a link in the upper right-hand corner of your iGoogle page.

To include iGoogle on your mobile phone, sign into your account, and click on the "get started" button under the "take iGoogle with you on your mobile phone" option. Google then walks you through three steps to add mobile-compatible gadgets that you want to view on your mobile device, edit steps to add gadgets and how they will appear on your phone, and then, finally, view iGoogle on your phone.

When you edit your page, you actually view a sample phone on Google's site and drag and drop the title bars to change their order. You can move or delete gadgets, then click on the "update preview" box to view your changes. Once you have your page in the correct order, click the "continue" button, where you are given instructions on how to view iGoogle on your phone through your phone's Internet browser and how to send the access link directly to your phone.

To send the link directly to your phone, select the highlighted blue hyperlink that reads "send link directly to your phone," then enter your ten-digit mobile phone number in the box (including dashes) and click on the "send" button. Google automatically sends a text message to your phone. Click on the link that you received from Google, which takes you directly to your iGoogle page. Note that Google does not charge for this service, but depending on your phone plan, your carrier may charge you for the text message you receive. Click the "OK" button to end the process on your computer.

Google Reader

Google Reader is a consolidation tool for bringing a user's favorite websites into one place. It uses RSS Feeds to continually update the content and can collect information from news sites, blogs, and other Web sources to customize your Web information experience. Adding subscriptions to Google

Reader for your customized information can be done by entering a Web address or by typing in a keyword for a topic of interest, and Google will make suggestions based on that keyword. You can then view headlines of each site, consolidate the information, or check out each site individually.

This service could be used to keep everyone in your company informed on relevant topics that affect your business. Also, if your ads appear on the Content Network, they could appear on these sites. This service is another way Google is attempting to promote relevant Web content. You can also use the sites that are offered through keyword search on Google Reader to manually target for your AdWords Content Network settings.

Using an RSS feed

RSS is an acronym for Really Simple Syndication. An RSS feed is indicated on a website or blog in the form of a round-edged, orange box with three white, rainbow-like lines. It can also be shown as icons with the name of the information source and a "plus" sign, or a button that says "XML" or "RSS."

Syndication in the media typically means that information is produced and then distributed through multiple channels. Examples of syndication are radio shows, television shows, cartoons, and newspaper columns. The "Dear Abby" newspaper column is an example of syndicated column because it is produced in one location and then widely distributed through newspapers, and now on websites. Syndications of this kind usually involve a fee for the information.

An RSS feed is similar in that it widely distributes information through different venues. The big difference is that RSS feeds are typically free and are distributed only on the Internet. Venues can include e-mail, Web portals, and news readers to mobile devices, desktops, or other Web-based devices. The information is distributed in a standard format and can be from news headlines, video, audio, podcasts, and blogs. Providers of content in the offline world are also major contributors to content through RSS feeds. Google is a publisher of a large number of feeds, as are major news channels such as ABC, BBC News, CBS, CNN, Fox News, MSNBC, the New York Times, NBC, USA Today, and the Washington Post. Many online magazines and blogs hosted by individuals also provide RSS feeds.

To set up your blog, website, photos, video, or audio content as an RSS feed for publication, multiple tools are available to translate Web content into the RSS distribution format. Many blog publishing tools, such as Blogger, TypePad®, and WordPress will allow you to publish your feeds automatically.

The benefit of RSS feeds to you, as an advertiser, is that it bypasses spam filters, is excluded from the search engine ranking process, and it is a cost-effective way to reach those interested in your products, services, and the activities of your organization continually. You can both provide feeds and advertise on them. Think of it as an online newsletter that can be updated on an hourly or minute-by-minute basis and instantly reaches a target audience that has already expressed interest in what you have to say.

The benefit of RSS feeds to subscribers is that the information is regularly delivered to you as it is updated, rather than requiring you to visit multiple sites that provide you with news and information on topics of interest. This also limits the information coming into your e-mail inbox, and it shrinks your time management challenges by allowing you to look at a lot of information quickly. You can check the feeds when you are ready to get more information, instead of saving lots of e-mails in your inbox until you are ready to read them.

To subscribe to an RSS feed, click the RSS icon on a site or blog that you would like to regularly receive updates from. RSS feed icons are typically found at the top or bottom of sites and blogs. Many sites also now include the RSS feed icon in the URL box for your Web browser.

Becoming a Google Advertising Professional

Being a qualified member of Google's Advertising Professionals Program gives you more credibility as you work to increase the client base of advertising clients. Being a member of the program shows you have proficiency in using AdWords, and you stay in the loop with updates and tips on how to use AdWords. Google provides a Google Advertising Professional logo that you can post on your site, and Google offers promotions, credits, and marketing tools to help bring in new clients, and better serve your existing client base. For AdWords advertisers that may only manage AdWords accounts for themselves, becoming a Google Advertising Professional by spending wisely and taking the exam can benefit you with the knowledge that you gain through taking the exam and through real world experience. One other benefit available through the Advertising Professionals Program includes the My Client Center interface, which allows you to manage multiple clients through one interface rather than sign in through multiple accounts.

How much does it cost?

Within the AdWords Learning Center, Google has included a Google Advertising Fundamentals Exam. You can access this exam through the "welcome to the AdWords Learning Center" page at **www.adwords.google. com/support**. According to Google, the lessons provided with the link include all the content you need to prepare for the exam. There is no cost for taking the exam and no fee for initially becoming recognized through this program, but a company must maintain a spending minimum over a 90-day period. These spending requirements vary by country, and are subject to change. As of this writing, the United States requirement is $10,000 spent over 90 days. This spending threshold must also be combined with proven experience that is demonstrated by the accounts being managed spending 60 days out of the 90-day period. If your spending drops below the threshold for 30 days, your status is revoked.

So, the company must be managing active accounts that spend a combined minimum amount. If a company is managing accounts that spend money two-thirds of the time and are managing the minimum spending requirement, your experience must be beyond the beginner level. The time and focus necessary to manage this type of spending with multiple accounts or one large account would qualify a company as experienced even without successfully completing exams. However, someone associated with your company is required to complete at least two exams successfully. These exams cannot be included on individual accounts, but must be on the same company account.

Note that there are qualified companies and qualified individuals. There is no minimum-spending requirement to become a qualified individual, but you must pass certification exams. You must pass the Google Advertising Fundamentals Exam — which should be easy to navigate because of the real-world experience you gain as a manager of this amount of spending — along with one of the advanced exams and agree to Google's terms and conditions. Google suggests that you take the exam after you have met the minimum time and spending requirements. There is no time limit for taking the exam, and you can tackle the text lessons provided in the Exam Learning Center at your own pace and in your own time.

Conclusion

Knowing your organization, goals, objectives, target audience, and message are vital to successfully planning any type of promotions, awareness, sales, or branding effort. With AdWords, launching a single campaign or a dozen campaigns with a focused message to a specific target audience is simple.

No matter what your level of expertise, or lack thereof, in the field of advertising, you can do this. And now, with the tools found throughout this book and the information about how to best use the tools found within AdWords, you are equipped to launch and more successfully maintain your own campaigns, or knowledgeably supervise an agency, individual, or department working on your behalf.

Keep in mind that even though the initial campaign launch process is simple and straightforward, there are many options for presenting your message through AdWords. Give yourself some time to ease into the world of AdWords. Then, as you understand more about how your organization can grow through AdWords, use all of the resources available. Refer back to the worksheets, quizzes, and examples included in this guide. They will help you stay grounded and focused on the purpose of your AdWords and other promotions efforts.

The creation, analysis, and optimization tools found throughout AdWords are included as part of the system. Use them all. As you become more familiar with the reports and information provided through AdWords, you will most likely find that you are gaining a greater understanding of your AdWords keywords, landing pages, and ads; you are also gaining a great understanding of how your target audience thinks. Integrating more information about your target audience into your current and future campaigns will make them stronger and more successful. Responding to the needs of your audience is imperative. Being able to anticipate those needs by your products, services, and message is invaluable.

Google has successfully outpaced its search engine competition, and, therefore, other search engine advertising programs, by responding to the core needs of its target audience. As Google focuses on how search results provide relevant information and options for users, it integrates this thought process into the efforts of its successful advertisers. Make it relevant. That is the basis for your success with keywords, landing pages, ads, and all of your other promotional and communications efforts, no matter what you are trying to sell, give away, or share with the world.

The AdWords system is relevant to you as an advertiser because it gives you the option to both limit and expand your world. It allows for some creativity and also offers forgiving tools for those not so creatively minded who also want to convey a professional, engaging message. It can also be relevant no matter the size of your budget.

You can spend as little or as much time working with AdWords as you want, but, keep in mind that optimizing your campaigns and gaining the biggest return on your AdWords investment does require monitoring. Once you get something to work, your competitor may step in and derail your rate of return. Of course, you also can do that with your competitors. With any business or organization, change is a certain thing. AdWords can change and adapt with you and for you as you meet the challenge of your competition, introduce new products and services, and adapt to the marketplace.

Hopefully, through understanding and using the ideas and instructions throughout this book, you can use AdWords to grow and strengthen your organization. Now get online, get to work and make 'em sell like hotcakes!

Appendix

Web site Resources

These references are provided to make it easier for you to grow your business. A listing here does not imply that any research has been done about the quality of these sites and their associated content, so compare the services and associated costs carefully before deciding to include their information in enhancing your organization's goals.

The Better Business Bureau® offers business resources on their sites, **www. bbb.org** and **www.bbbonline.org,** to equip businesses of all sizes and types to conduct business in an ethical and trustworthy manner including:

- alerts
- tips
- training
- a video library
- tax center
- and more

Blog software

For software to create and maintain a blog, compare the features and benefits of these sites:

- **www.blogger.com**: a free publishing tool offered by Google

- **www.blogit.com**: a paid blogging site that supports the bloggers who participate in the group

- **www.hubpages.com**: a free blogging site that offers a community of writers to work with and potential paid blogging opportunities.

- **www.squarespace.com**: a paid site that offers you the opportunity to design a website and blog in a stylish way

- **www.typepad.com**: a paid site that offers a free-trial period and a community of writers who can help you improve your blog

- **www.wordpress.org**: free site designed for bloggers. WordPress has evolved into a place where you can customize your page to do almost anything.

Bibliography

Goodman, Andrew. *Winning Results with Google AdWords.* 2nd Ed. Mc-Graw-Hill Osborne Media, 2009.

Harris, Daniel. *Adwords 100 Success Secrets: Google Adwords Secrets Revealed, How to Get the Most Sales Online, Increase Sales, Lower CPA and Save Time and Money.* Emereo Pty Limited, 2008.

Jacobson, Howie, Ph.D. *AdWords for Dummies.* New Jersey: Wiley Publishing, Inc., 2007.

Marshall, Perry, and Todd, Bryan. *Ultimate Guide to Google AdWords: How to Access 100 Million People in 10 Minutes.* Entrepreneur Media, Inc., 2007.

Misner, Harry J. *The Best Damn Google AdWords Book: Maximize Your Results to Maximize Your Advertising Dollars.* Rev. Ed. CreateSpace, 2008.

Smith, Jon. *Google AdWords That Work: 7 Secrets for Cashing in With the World's No. 1 Search Engine.* United Kingdom: The Infinite Ideas Company Limited, 2009.

Stokes, Richard. *Mastering Search Advertising: How the Top 3% of Search Advertisers Dominate Google AdWords.* Indiana: iUniverse, Inc., 2008.

Author Biography

Larisa Lambert writes, edits, and consults on advertising, marketing, publishing and business endeavors, and strategy. She also develops and manages business, communications, training, and promotions projects. As a partner in her family's business since 1997, she has helped it grow from an idea to one of the largest privately held companies of its kind in her home state of Alabama.

Lambert's favorite projects have included product launches, training organizations to communicate effectively with employees and markets, and working with individuals to make the most of their abilities. Helping people and businesses one-by-one see and reach their potential and maximize their contribution for themselves, organizations, and society is her passion.

She also loves driving with the windows down when it is cold, finding out what people *really* think, singing at the top of her lungs, laughing with her three boys, talking to strangers, and dessert.

Index

288 The Complete Guide to Google AdWords